# YOU TOLD ME TO BE BRAVE

Even while tripping over life's edges, her love kept him walking.

A memoir by

Mohan Mathew Chacko

ISBN: 978-93-343-9725-3

Cover & Interior Design: Designed by the author, incorporating an AI-generated visual.

Published by: The Author

First Edition, 2025

## TABLE OF CONTENTS

## DEDICATION:

To my mother who left too soon, but never truly left.
You held my hand through the earliest chapters of my life.
This book is my way of holding yours through the rest.
**Mariamma Chacko**

MOHAN MATHEW CHACKO

## FOREWORD

**By Mathew George Chandy**
CEO, Bangalore Hospice Trust – Karunashraya
*Karunashraya provides free palliative care to advanced-stage cancer patients who are beyond cure.*
https://karunashraya.org/

This is not a book that sets out to dazzle.

It does something far rarer—it invites us to listen, quietly, to a son remembering his mother.

The words that follow were not meant for an audience at first.

They began as fragments, private recollections nudged awake by the innocent questions of a daughter. Yet from those fragments has emerged a memoir at once deeply personal and unexpectedly universal.

To lose a mother in childhood is to inherit both absence and resilience.

The author does not present his story as a grand narrative or a polished arc, but as moments—snapshots in which grief and laughter, bewilderment and endurance, are allowed to coexist. It is in this very ordinariness, rendered with honesty and restraint that the extraordinary resides.

As someone who has spent years alongside patients and families living with advanced cancer, I know well how memory persists even when life is shortened, how love continues to guide even when presence is withdrawn.

Reading these pages, I was reminded that while death interrupts, it does not conclude. A mother's influence does not vanish; it becomes woven into the very fabric of those left behind.

What struck me most in this memoir is its gentleness.

There are no claims to wisdom, no dramatic gestures—only the steady unfolding of a boyhood shaped by both rupture and resilience.

In sharing this story, the author gives voice to countless unspoken experiences: of children who grieve in silence, of families who stumble forward, of love that lingers in the small details—a favourite meal, a fleeting memory, a word too tender to say aloud.

This book will not tell you how to grieve.

It will simply remind you that grief, when held and honoured, becomes part of who we are.

And it will remind you, as it reminded me, that the word "Mum," whispered across time, is never lost.

**Mathew George Chandy**

## PREFACE

I didn't set out to write a book.

I set out to remember.

And somewhere along the way, those memories... once scattered like old boarding school report cards... began forming something more coherent. Not quite a life story, but a life seen from the quiet corner of hindsight.

It started with my daughter asking me a perfectly ordinary question.

I can't recall what it was—something about my school days or my favourite childhood meal. But the answer didn't come easily. Not because I had forgotten, but because I had tucked so much of it away. That moment made me pause. And that pause grew into pages.

This is a memoir of childhood—of loss, laughter, longing, and the curious ways children make sense of things they can't fully understand. It's not a linear journey. More like a series of snapshots from a boy's world turned upside down by one devastating absence, and steadied—however imperfectly—by the people and places that followed.

There are no great life lessons here, no dramatic climaxes or wisecracks delivered with cinematic flair. Just the quiet unfolding of a boy trying to grow up while holding onto something he couldn't keep.

In the process of writing, I found myself talking more openly to my daughter about things I had never voiced. She may not realise it, but she helped unlock this story, without meaning to, and mostly by asking innocent questions at the wrong time (like just when I had settled down for a nap).

This book isn't about her. But it is, in a way, because of her.

If you've ever found yourself unexpectedly emotional over a long-forgotten memory… or caught off guard by the sound of your own voice saying, "My mother used to…"—then perhaps this book will find a place with you.

It's about grief, yes. But also about resilience, omelettes, cousins, confusion, and the things we carry long after we've stopped mentioning them.

Above all, it's about the word I went silent on for far too long.

Mum.

## ACKNOWLEDGEMENTS

Writing a memoir is a strange journey—some days like lifting a veil, other days like folding fog into a box. Heavy memories and stubborn sentences weighed me down, yet every struggle shaped these pages into something alive.

I am grateful to my brother **Mathew Thomas**, whose sharp eye and steady critiques strengthened this book—even when his "help" nearly made me throw my pen at the wall. To my friend **Vasu Murti**, who taught me that balance isn't just a yoga pose. From wandering conversations about life to thoughtful feedback on this memoir, he kept me grounded and moving forward. To **Shoba Chandy**, for encouragement—and for persuading her husband, **Mathew George Chandy**, to write the Foreword to this book. With years guiding palliative care centres, and first-hand encounters with terminally ill patients and their families, he brings depth and humanity to that reflection, a perspective that resonates with the journey I shared with my mother through breast cancer and a brain tumour.

To **my cousins**, who shared memories of my mother that stitched light through darker reflections. To **J.C. George**, Ichayan, who was among the first to call with encouragement when I began this memoir, reminding me with his storyteller's eye that even ordinary lives can belong on life's screen.

To my daughter **Maria** and her husband **Joel**, who saw the struggle close up, offering critique and comfort. And to **Polly**, my wife—your quiet patience and faith steadied me when I faltered.

And to **my parents**, whose presence I still feel in every photograph and memory—this memoir belongs to them as much as to me.

**No writer walks this path alone**. If these pages hold any truth, it is because of every gesture, every word, every hand that reminded me my story mattered—and that remembering and sharing can itself be a quiet courage.

## Prologue

Some stories begin at the end.

This one begins in a graveyard. With the sound of small stones hitting a coffin lid. With the voice of a ten-year-old boy still hoping for a miracle. Hoping that if he wished hard enough, the woman in that box... the one who knew all his fears and all his favourite foods... would rise, smile, and say, "Let's go home."

She didn't. And yet, in a quiet and persistent way, she never quite left either

She lived on... in the sacred weekend omelette, in the rules about curry leaves and toothpaste, in the silent stares that made even older cousins behave at breakfast. She lingered in the background of every new school admission, every exam hall, and every boarding school letter read with trembling fingers. She surfaced in my conscience each time I laughed at a prank, craved an old toy, or secretly judged my father's silences.

Especially later, when those silences gave way to something new... a woman stepping into our home, soft-spoken but sure. The same woman my Mummy had once, almost gently, said Daddy would marry when she was gone.

I remembered that moment only much later... the way children do, storing things they don't yet understand. I didn't know how to feel. There was no warning bell. Just a sense of being slowly erased from a picture I couldn't stop drawing.

This is not merely a story of loss. It is the story of slow dawning... from the wide-eyed denial of a child who thought prayers could reverse death, to the reluctant understanding that not all departures come with goodbyes.

It is also the story of a young boy learning the shapes of sorrow in unfamiliar places... through shifting cities, changing languages, pranks by seniors, and longing for a home-cooked meal while clutching tins of broken biscuits in a lonely dormitory.

It was a time when advanced medicine was a distant promise, when even the word "cancer" felt foreign.

And yet, I watched my mother transform—from the most enchanting and dependable presence in my life into the fiercest, most unyielding woman I have ever known.

She fought breast cancer. And then, a brain tumour.

And still, she mothered.

What follows is an uneven dance between levity and grief.

There are moments of wild laughter and sugar mountains. Of appams served with maternal pride. Of acrobatics in hospital canteens. Of cousins who were heroes one moment, and mysterious beings the next.

These stories will make you smile... sometimes even as your throat tightens.

But beneath it all, there is a growing emotional intelligence... a child slowly recognising that grown-ups hurt too. That faith can't always fix things. That guilt can be born not of wrongdoing, but of helplessness. That missing someone isn't an event; it's a condition you carry.

Mummy was the axis around which my world spun. Her absence did not stop the spinning. It just made everything wobble.

If you've ever lost someone before you had the words to describe what that meant... or if you've ever tried to grow up while holding tightly to someone you couldn't keep... then perhaps these pages will echo something in you.

I was told to be brave. What remains now is the long arc of goodbye. And I'm still learning how.

## PASSAGE 1: MUM'S THE WORD

Hushed Reflections on Loss and Hope

The warm noon sun is beating down on me, casting a bright shine over the rows of tombstones.

The grass is dry and yellowed, crunching underfoot as I make my way through the maze of graves.

The air is thick with the scent of flowers, both fresh and wilted, placed in the loving memory of those who have passed.

The occasional breeze brings with it the rustling of leaves and the creaking of nearby trees.

The distant hum of a car engine reminds me that the world outside this place is still going on. But here, in the graveyard, time seems to stand still.

The silence is occasionally interrupted by the hushed voices of mourners. People who've come to remember those they've lost. To reflect on their lives and to feel a connection with them once again.

So much time has moved on. Yet those poignant memories remain vivid.

***

Mummy's body is being lowered into the grave. With relatives and friends gathered around.

I'm confused and overwhelmed. I am trying to decipher the chants and prayers. Confused with all the religious procedures and ceremonial activities.

My cousin pushes some sand onto my palm and urges me with a compulsive expression in his eyes. I'm feeling reluctant to throw sand on her body.

My 10-year-old timid brain imagines that she would be in discomfort if sand fell on her relaxed, sleeping face.

I instinctively obey, though reluctantly. The moment the sand falls on my mom's body, I painfully grimace.

The small stones in the sand strike the wooden coffin in a distressing splatter.

I'm dismayed at the insensitive nature of this procedure.

Wasn't it difficult enough to die?

I visualise her accepting the sand dropped on her as the absolute confirmation of my having cast away all hope of her coming back alive.

I could almost hear her saying, 'Son, how could you do this to me?'

I'm harbouring this strong secret sentiment in the inner recesses of my mind that I am about to witness a miracle since I am praying strongly for her.

I am trustingly hoping she wakes from her sleep all hale and hearty. Especially since the priests are repeatedly chanting a verse imploring God to renew the dead person.

And I'm waiting. Waiting for the miracle to come.

My hopes of my mom coming back to life are dashed when they proceed to close the grave with the concrete slabs. I feel a twinge of guilt that my prayers weren't strong enough.

God seems unwilling to give my mom a fresh lease on life.

I'm still determined to persistently hope that all that's happening around me would go away like a bad dream. All I want now is to open my eyes to find Mom's smiling face appreciating my earnest prayers.

I eventually walk out of the cemetery disoriented and dejected.

I'm still perplexed at why such apparent indulgence in spiritual chants and ceremonial practices has failed to bring back my mom.

***

The church bells bring me back to the present.

Memories. Memories. Memories.

The sands of time have been falling. Slipping through my fingers, and now my heart's gone numb.

I pass by rows of headstones on the graves, each one a tribute to a life now passed on to the other side. Adorned with flowers, trinkets, and burnt candles… quenched in the wind.

A sense of comfort washes over me. No place anchors you to the past, present, and future like a cemetery.

## PASSAGE 2: WALK THROUGH MEMORY LANE

A Serene Escape to the Church with Mom in Bustling Calcutta

It's 1964. Calcutta is buzzing and vibrant.

Saturdays are special for us. It's the day when I have Mummy totally for myself.

I'm almost 4 years old. And it's the day we take a stroll to the Church in the morning.

I'm holding her hand tightly as we navigate the streets. With rickshaws, bicycles, and buses jostling for scarce tarmac space.

So off we go. I'm dapper in a shirt and shorts. Mummy, elegant in her crisply pleated saree.

Oh boy, walking! It's great for the first few minutes. I'm all charged up with "Yes, let's go explore the world!" but after a few minutes, it's more like "Oh boy, when are we reaching?" So yeah, you could say I'm not exactly a walking enthusiast.

On the other hand, my Mummy is a walking encyclopaedia. She's the smartest person in the whole world. How else can she know the answer to every question I can think of?

And she explains it all in such detail that I feel like I'm getting both entertained and illuminated in whatever topic I'm fascinated by.

And she doesn't just stop at answering. She looks right into my eyes to make sure I'm satisfied with her response.

Of course, I always am – she's a genius! It's like she's on a mission to make me the smartest kid in the world.

***

We eventually reach the stretch of the street where the sounds get quieter. Not many more street vendors.

After a multitude of those faceless vendors, I am approaching my favourite place. The textile shop of Sardarji Uncle.

We've never bought anything from his shop, but Sardarji Uncle always waves at me like we're old friends.

He sits high up among towers of colourful cloth, his big white beard like a fluffy cloud and his shiny steel bangle flashing in the light.

One day, Mummy even let me go right up to him. I shook his hand—it was warm, a bit scratchy, and smelled like the cloth in his shop. I felt like I'd just made friends with a king.

***

Removed from the noise and chaos, the church is located in a pocket of beauty and calm. It feels like a cozy, happy little bubble where everything is still.

We spend some time in silence, kneeling in prayer. I share some thoughts with God. Things that I think he had better know. And very soon run out of topics.

I prefer talking to Mom.

I steal a glance at her from the corner of my eye. She is in deep prayer and thought. And I dare not interrupt such moments of silence.

After a while, she is showing signs of finishing her prayer.

Her smile indicates that she's content. She's happy about my not interrupting her session with God. And her loving smile embraces me.

Mom has a way with words.

She's often talking about God through stories and examples. And I love those narrations and descriptions.

Yet for me, my Mom fulfils the profile of God.

All that I ever wanted, I could receive from her. All that I need, as if by some kind of sixth sense, she would provide me even before I realise it myself.

I like God because Mom likes God.

I respect God because my Mom asks me to.

I am happy in my little world, unaware of anything beyond that. Because I know that my Mom is always there for me, no matter what.

Just that there is no way I can see that fate has made a booking on an exclusive rollercoaster experience of turmoil and pain, a few years from now.

## Passage 3: The Belly Worshipper of 63, Karaya Road, Calcutta

Saturday Strolls, Delicacy Calls

Yay, we're all done with praying. And it's time to leave the Church.

I instinctively follow Mummy toward the offering box. And swiftly dig into my shorts' pocket for the shiny coin Mummy had entrusted me with. Huge relief! It's still safely hiding in the corner of my pocket's seam.

My coin clinks when it joins the other coins in the offering box.

So, that's done. And I turn to seek Mummy's smile of approval.

Mummy is already at the door. Beaming at me with pride.

Mummy ties my shoelaces so well. Never too tight. My feet feel snug and cozy.

So now we stride towards the parish priest.

He's sitting in his wicker chair on the grassy green patch facing the parsonage in the Church compound.

He rises and welcomes us with an infectious, charismatic smile. Dignity and grace writ large all over his clean-shaven face.

I pull myself up into an empty wicker chair next to him.

"I am four years old", I tell him with much aplomb.

It's my favourite opening line nowadays. The world needs to realise that they're dealing with a grown-up guy now.

"Yes, that's great", he confirms.

I'm revelling in his undivided attention. And gladly answering all his courtesy questions to impress Mummy.

Mummy is smiling appreciatively. So I'm on the right track.

As we speak, I can't help but notice the enticing smell of food wafting toward us.

All that aroma of street food we encountered on our way to Church has juiced up a ravenous appetite in me. And the tantalising whiff wafting from the mess hall is not making life easier.

My head is uncontrollably tilting towards the entrance to the mess hall. And I'm practically salivating. My good manners and patience are crumbling to fragments.

And Mummy seems to know exactly what's happening.

She begins to rise from her chair, asking for permission to leave. And my hopes of having food from there start to crack like eggshells.

But God intervenes. And makes the priest insist that we stay for a little while more. And guides me toward the mess hall.

And I'm feeling like I'm being led into heaven.

Mummy is politely trying her best to decline this offer. But her best isn't good enough.

I know better than to look at Mummy's face now. So I hold on tight to my saviour's hand and focus on what's important.

Focus, Hocus, Pocus!

In a few minutes, I'm diving into the world's fluffiest and yummiest omelette.

***

On the way back home, we're on a different route. Mummy wants to meet a friend on the way.

I'm holding tight to the sides of the rickshaw as it swerves to avoid a stray dog.

I must ask Mummy if I can be a rickshaw driver when I grow a little taller. Someday, I too shall wield this pedal-powered chariot through these streets. And jostle past fruit carts, and zip through tiny gaps between cars.

***

We reach Mummy's friend's house while I'm still enjoying the thrill of the ride.

A cheerful lady greets us. She seems more like my friend than my Mom's. And is eager to feed me everything she has in the house. My profile makes it easy to guess that I have an inclination toward food.

Succulent Rosogollas keep coming.

And I keep digging into these spongy white delights, unconscious of space and time.

When I'm past a couple of servings, Mummy nudges me out of my sugar-induced stupor.

Mummy is sitting on the chair's edge, spine straight as a pencil. And staring into my face.

She's not falling for my feigned innocence and sugar-syrup smile.

She retains her smile while her friend keeps assuring me in affectionate Bengali that she's got more of those in the kitchen. And she's patting my head in reassurance.

But the air is heavy with Mummy's glare, making it hard for me to breathe with a swollen belly.

***

Once back home at 63, Karaya Road, I'm longing for the next Saturday to come.

Who knows what kinds of delicacies await us along the way!

## Passage 4: Dripping With Liquid Happiness

Why I love Aunts and not Uncles

Mummy's left me in the house of a family friend. And one of the hosts is unfriendly, unsmiling, and unrelenting.

I'm at Titus Uncle and Aunty's house for the day.

Uncle has his head buried in the newspaper.

He's playing hard-to-get.

I want to say hello and shake hands like Mummy has taught me. But from what I can see, his Mummy hasn't taught him good manners.

That's fine by me because my friend is Aunty anyway.

She not only shakes my hand but also gives me a warm hug smelling of freshly baked cookies.

She's gratified to watch me lick my lips after I devour the cookies placed before me.

And now that the plate is empty, I open the new Tom and Jerry comic book that Mummy bought me. Books are so much fun when they have the "new" smell.

I'm engrossed in the thrill of the chase with Tom and Jerry. And the newspaper rustles as Uncle finally folds the paper and drops it on the table.

From the corner of my eye, I notice him inching toward me. Like Tom stealthily moves toward Jerry in my book.

He clears his throat noisily, and our conversation commences.

"What's your name?" He asks.

"My name is Mohan Mathew Chacko."

That's how I must say my name to elders (According to Mummy).

"Where are you from?"

"I live at 63 Karaya Road, Calcutta," I answer with well-practised confidence.

"But where are you from?"

Now, I'm fumbling for words. And Aunty smiles. She prompts me to tell Uncle where my native place is.

"I'm from Kerala".

"Oh, so you're a Carolinian?" he asks in his jaunty, stylish manner.

"I'm from Kerala". I repeat in a slow modulation so that the poor man can read my lips.

"So are you a Keralian or a Keralite?"

Aunty blinks her eyes at me discreetly. Uncle is relentlessly striving to get to know my roots.

Once and for all, I reassure him – "I'm from Kerala".

***

Later, exuding an air of condescension, Uncle goes off for a short nap. And Aunty vanishes into the kitchen.

Left to my own devices, I look around for something to entertain myself.

That's a cute little bottle on the shelf.

I'm impressed by its feel and texture. So I give it a little squeeze. And a fragrant liquid squirts out.

Wow! I've always wanted something like this.

So I scurry across to the verandah and squeeze it again, and the liquid squirts out in a stream. The more I squeeze, the more it shoots out.

So I refill the bottle with water and squirt it on the plants. And repeat the process until all the plants get watered well. And their leaves drip with liquid happiness.

I'm happy for the plants and Aunty.

Now that I have saved her the trouble of watering her plants, I'm pretty sure that Aunty will give me some more cookies as a reward for my responsible actions.

And as evidence of my hard work, I show her the empty bottle.

She gasps with bulging eyes.

Then, lowering her voice to a whisper, she confides that the bottle had contained Uncle's expensive medicine.

While I'm still struggling with the daunting immensity of the situation, I'm flinching at the thought of what Mummy is going to say.

Aunty reads my mind, and says – "This will be our little secret".

Greatly relieved, I give Aunty a tight hug. And the smell of cookies makes me hungry again.

***

Back home, while I tuck myself into bed, Mummy reads out a story from my book of 365 Bedtime Stories.

Little does she know that there's a thrilling story that Titus Aunty and I have kept to ourselves.

## PASSAGE 5: ADIEU, DEAR CALCUTTA

Future-pull of our native place

The doorbell chimes. And I am jolted. Shaken back into the real world from my storybook world.

Mummy stops knitting and walks across to open the door. We know it is Daddy coming back from work.

I run across to Daddy and hug him. And I'm greeted by the warmth of his big, wide smile and the smell of cigarettes.

I take care not to crush the pack of Berkeley Cigarettes in Daddy's shirt pocket. I need them in good condition once they are empty. For my collection.

My stack of cigarette packs is neatly organised on my windowsill. Everyone who comes into my room is impressed. But somehow Mummy doesn't get it.

Daddy is always exhausted when he reaches home.

Mummy says Daddy's job is very tiring. She isn't too happy with Daddy not becoming a lawyer.

Daddy studied law but doesn't want to practice law.

Recently, Daddy has been advocating the advantages of starting a business in Kerala, our native place.

And Mummy, though not studied in law, has become a pleader. Pleading with Daddy not to resign from his job.

Mummy loves Kerala but only wants to visit.

She likes living and working in Calcutta. And cannot imagine getting uprooted from here.

I'm on Mummy's side. Because I too don't want to leave Calcutta and lose my friends.

Life here is full of wonder and excitement, and I am blessed to have so many friends to share it with.

It's always one birthday party after another. All of us get to meet each other so many times for our birthdays.

I'm happy and loved. And surrounded by so much celebration and joy.

And in between all these good times, I cannot understand why Daddy is longing for a change.

When it comes to Mummy, stability is everything. Everything she chooses for herself and her family has been run through her mind with clarity of purpose.

It is always long-term benefits for Mummy. Nothing fancy. Never swayed by fads and trends.

For instance, her shopping list is ironclad and with very limited scope for flexibility. Cinthol soap, Forhans Toothpaste, Cuticura powder, and so on. These are what we use, and these are what we buy. Nothing more, nothing less.

I once attempted to get her attention to a magazine ad for an attractive red and white striped "Signal" toothpaste.

She listened to my point of view without interruption and then gave me a firm smile. And explained why our Forhans toothpaste was the best for us.

I tried grumbling that it didn't foam and that it didn't give a fresh and tangy feel like other toothpaste. But I knew better than to persist in messing with her well-thought-out choices.

And I am wondering how Daddy's disruptive plans can ever be acceptable to a person like Mummy. Clearly, some things are beyond my comprehension.

After a while, Daddy comes after a bath smelling of, of course, Cinthol soap. And we nibble through dinner without anyone uttering a word.

That night, Mummy explained to me during bedtime that we must always be in a state of gratitude to God for the good friends He gives us at each juncture of our lives. And that nothing lasts forever.

And I'm startled at the bland finality of having to leave my birthplace.

***

And one day in December 1964, we say goodbye to Calcutta and take a train to Kerala.

We're leaving behind many friends with whom we share great memories.

Daddy says we'll be back someday. Mummy shrugs half-heartedly while staring out the window, lost in thought.

The train chugs loudly as if to fill the silent emptiness in our hearts.

## Passage 6: Country Boats, Take Me Home

Transitioning in transit

Our train is a big, loud monster, roaring and rumbling as it zooms along.

Outside my window, dark shadows play games, twisting and twirling around.

I squint and strain my eyes to figure out what is happening out there. But there's nothing but the darkness of the night.

But hey, I've got a better idea.

Let me snuggle up to Mummy's side. And boy, is she warm and cozy! Her confident smile keeps me calm and cheerful during these crazy times.

This is my second adventure on the train to Kerala.

The first time, I was just a baby. I don't remember a thing. But thanks to our super family album, those memories are like hidden treasures waiting to be discovered.

Mummy is the one behind it all, with her captions filling in the blanks and making the stories come to life.

At home, every now and then, we bring out the album. And it's like unlocking a treasure chest of happiness. We travel back in time and relive those amazing moments frozen in the pictures.

But you know what I'm super excited about? I can't wait to meet all my cousins, Aunts, Uncles, and especially Granny. We're going to have so much fun together.

Get ready, guys, here I come, full speed ahead on the fastest train in the world!

Grandparents are the most precious people in the world. But sadly, I only have one grandparent who is still alive. Mummy tells me that life can be unfair sometimes, but we learn to adapt and keep going.

Mummy, her sisters and brother learned this lesson in a difficult way when Grandma and Grandpa passed away when they were very young.

But they didn't give up. They faced all their challenges and remained strong for one another.

Daddy, on the other hand, lost his father while he was away at college.

So I am happy and grateful for the one grandparent I have.

Until now, I've only seen pictures of Granny and relied on my imagination to create memories. But tomorrow evening, we will reach our ancestral home, and I can start making real memories with Granny. And I can't wait!

***

*"Chai, chaaaai! Kaapi kaaapee!"*

The Tea and Coffee vendors at the railway station shout so loudly, it startles me from my sleep!

I don't even drink tea or coffee. Still, I'm super excited! Guess why?

Because Mummy told me that today, we're allowed to buy food from the stations.

The food she packed from home is delicious — lemon rice, spicy mango pickle, and crunchy papad.

But eating food from railway stations is not an everyday thing, you know? It's like a special treat!

There's something about the clatter of wheels, the warm breeze, and those sing-song vendor calls...

*"Vada paav, samose, garam garam!"*

I press my nose against the window bars, eyes scanning for the food carts. The aroma hits me before the food does.

I want to stand on the platform with Daddy and maybe even meet the train driver. But no way! Mummy tells me to go back to sleep.

So I snuggle up against her soft skin instead.

***

Oh boy, we finally make it to Kottayam. And we hop into a taxi to go to Thiruvarppu, our village.

As we drive, everything around us is so green and beautiful.

Coconut trees swaying in the breeze, lush green fields, and ponds beside the road. We even pass by a river that's sparkling green!

The taxi slows down as we approach a small, narrow bridge. And the moment we drive onto it, the whole thing starts creaking and groaning like some part of it is getting loose and might fall off any second.

**"Creeeak... clank... creeeak..."**

I grip the edge of the seat. Is this bridge planning to hold us up... or plop us into the water?

But everyone seems calm. The driver is smiling. Mummy is calmly enjoying the scenery. And then she catches my eye and gives me a smile that says, "It's all good, son!"

She leans over and says, "This is the Illickal Bridge."

Honestly, I was expecting a name like The Bridge of Doom.

Finally, we arrive at our village, and guess how we're going to get home? On a country boat! Cars can't reach our place because there are no fancy roads.

While our baggage is being loaded in, we get into the awesome wooden country boat that has been sent by Granny to fetch us.

I wonder how quickly this boat can take us to Granny. I'm sure she must be waiting eagerly.

## PASSAGE 7: CALCUTTA TO THIRUVARPPU - WORLDS APART

Our house by the stream

This new world is amazing!

The trees are dancing, and the boats are gliding. And Mummy expects me to sit all cool and calm.

How can I, when there's so much awesomeness all around?

Calcutta was such a happening and bustling place. And here in Thiruvarppu, it's so calm and peaceful.

This is such a huge change in our lives.

I'm right in the middle of the boat, safely away from the edge, just like Mummy said.

She warns me to close my mouth, or flies would zoom right in. Oopsie, I didn't realise my mouth and eyes were wide open!

And hey, take a look at the boatman. He's wearing a lungi tied super tightly to his waist. No shirt, no vest, no shoes, nothing!

My mouth starts to open wide in astonishment, but I catch myself just in time.

I know Mummy's got her eyes on me, even when she seems to be looking somewhere else.

Then, the man steps onto the boat and grabs this super-long yellow pole right next to it. He sticks one end of the pole into the water and pushes the boat away from the riverbank. That's how our river adventure begins.

Our boat moves silently, except for the splashy sound of water each time the pole goes in, and the thud it makes against the side of the boat.

Oh, and check out those green plants floating lazily in the water. Mummy says they're called "African *Paayal*" (floating aquatic ferns).

We soon cross a wide stretch of water and enter a narrow part of the river.

There are women and kids in front of the houses on both sides. They all seem to know Daddy.

Our boat glides so slowly, it's perfect for quick and fun conversations with everyone.

During the chat, their attention starts to shift toward me, and I give them the most polite smile ever.

Mummy's doing the same. We're like a team, spreading happiness everywhere we go. As long as I follow her lead, everything's easy-peasy.

Everyone knows everyone here, and they're all so happy and relaxed.

And guess what? I'm the only one bursting with uncontrollable excitement in this whole place. Mummy's keeping a close eye on me, making sure I don't go overboard with all the fun.

I wish my friends back in Calcutta could see me now, surrounded by all this greenery and nature. They'd be so jealous!

Finally, I can make out that we are reaching our ancestral home.

A few country boats of different sizes lie tied to trees. And my cousin sees us from a distance and calls out – "Valliammacheee!!"

He's letting Granny know that we're here.

By the time the boat gets docked on the side, we are greeted by my cousins and my Aunt. There are so many people, and I'm confused about where to look. And I'm clinging on to Mummy's saree for comfort.

We walk beside a mountain of coconuts gathered together into a big heap.

And as we step into the inner compound, the wooden doorway frames Granny's graceful presence.

She's wearing her traditional white attire.

Granny's mundu is folded into pleats like a paper fan to fit around the waist.

I can't help but run towards her and give her the tightest hug. The scent of oil on her body feels so strange yet comforting. It's like a warm embrace in itself.

But you know what catches my attention the most? Granny's earrings! They're round and as thick as my fingers, dangling from her ear lobes that have a big roundish gap. They sway with every movement, shining and sparkling.

I can't take my eyes off them. They're like little treasures hanging from Granny's ears, making her look even more magical.

Everyone is so excited and talking to each other all at once.

But what really catches my attention are the two short and hefty dogs. They wag their tails intensely but politely keep their distance.

And there's another big dog in a cage, barking ferociously. I think he is angry that he has to be in the cage when the other dogs are allowed to roam freely.

As I glance around, I see hens and ducks strutting around carefree and happy, exploring the surroundings and pecking at things. And a cow is crying out from somewhere nearby. She sounds like she's hungry.

That reminds me. I wonder what's there to eat. The minute I look at Mummy, she knows what I'm thinking.

Luckily, on the dining table, a few plates are piled up with snacks and sweets I've never seen before. Granny and my Aunty have made Kerala delicacies with fancy names such as *Kuzhalappam*, *Achappam*, and *Churuttu*.

I slyly whisper to Mom, "Can I have some Rosogollas?"

She smiles and explains that in Kerala, the delicacies are different from those in Calcutta.

Granny's home is like a world of its own. I've got cousins of all sizes, from big to small, and they're roaming around like little explorers. They don't need permission to have fun. It's so amazing!

And just when I thought things couldn't get crazier, I hear my cousins screaming by the riverbank.

And then, **BAM**! A thunderous splash echoes through the air!

I can't resist the temptation to find out what the hullabaloo is all about.

So, I put on my best puppy dog eyes and beg Mummy for permission to investigate.

But oh no, she's not falling for it! She knows better than to let a little adventurer like me wander off alone.

So it's going to be a case for the dynamic duo. The curious kid and the cautious Mom!

## PASSAGE 8: FREEDOM UNTIL MIDNIGHT

More action than I can stomach in a day

Oh boy, I'm in such a hurry! I've got to wash my hands and go faster than a rocket to solve the mystery of that sound.

But I can't find a wash basin anywhere! Maybe I should've just wiped my hands on my shorts like my cool cousin does.

Wait, what's this? Mummy points me to a shiny brass thing filled with water, sitting out on the verandah. She pours some water from it onto my hand, and I run super-fast.

Uh-oh, Mummy is right behind me. Time is slipping away. I can't waste a single moment!

Look, look! My cousins and some other cool kids from the neighbourhood are turning into daredevil divers, leaping off the super-high walk bridge. They go swooshing through the air, and when they hit the water, it makes the most gigantic splash ever! It's like **BOOM**!

I really, really want to dive right in and join the splish-splash party.

Mummy gives me the green light to stand on the lower steps with the water tickling my knees. Unfortunately, Mummy's voice has that serious "no more" tone.

So I guess a little splash is better than nothing. It's a good start, after all.

Oh my! Just when we're having a big splash, my Aunty declares it is time to end the crazy splashing because it is getting dark. My cousin tries to argue, but Mummy joins Aunty. And now the message is clear to everyone—no more swimming.

So, one by one, we reluctantly crawl out of the water like soggy little tortoises. And try to grab the only two towels lying around. We pass them around, trying to dry off all five of us at once. It's a towel-sharing extravaganza!

Hey, hold on a minute, all this action has made me hungry.

But Mummy says dinner won't be ready for a while.

***

As the darkness sets in, the sky fills with long and hurried chirps and tweets. Birds of all shapes and sizes take flight, forming their little groups up above.

It's funny how the hens scramble and perch on a tree next to the cow shed. My cousin tells me that the branches of this tree are the favourite night-time resting place of all our hens.

And after a while, the place gets eerily quiet.

No more dragonflies whirling through the air, no more squirrels running along the fence, no more bird calls.

All that remains is a light breeze ruffling the leaves.

I'm thinking, why doesn't anyone flip a switch and light up this darkness?

And then, aha! I spot some fancy brass lamps, big and small, being carefully placed in the rooms and the porch. It's like we've entered a magical kingdom of oil lamps.

The burning oil fills the air with a peculiar smell. It's a fragrant mystery!

Mummy says that electricity hasn't reached our village or the surrounding ones. Oh, so that's why we have so many oil lamps!

Dressed in comfy home clothes and still feeling hungry, I'm following my cousin everywhere he goes. He's my trusted guide now. And I feel safer when he's around, especially with all those lizards on every wall.

He tells me I should just ignore them. They're there to catch flies, that's all.

But I don't like how some of those big ones stare at me.

We wander around the house while he tells me cool things we can do tomorrow. That's great, but right now my main focus is dinner.

The appealing smells are pulling me toward the kitchen.

It's a huge kitchen. But there are too many people doing too many things there. So I'd better get out of the way.

My cousin has a secret plan to satisfy our hungry bellies. But we have to keep it super-secret.

He takes me up a creaky wooden stairway, and my heart beats louder than my rumbling tummy. We're on a secret mission and have to be super quiet.

He pushes up a wooden hatch that blocks the attic. With caution, he enters the attic while I wait on the last step, holding a small torch out for him.

He grabs a handful of bananas from one of the many bunches hanging from the low ceiling, and we fill our tummies until we have too many banana skin peels to handle.

We sneak out to the cowshed after closing the hatch and leave the banana peels in front of the cows.

From there, I catch a distant glimpse of a girl singing a wondrous tune.

Peeking across the stream, I see our neighbour's house, where a big brass lamp shines.

My cousin explains that the melody I'm hearing is a Hindu prayer chant. It's so strangely soothing, with its peaceful rhythm.

Just then, Granny calls all the kids for prayers.

So we sneak back into the house.

Granny sits on a mat rolled out on the verandah floor.

The light from the brass lamp brings a warm glow to our faces. She reads from her big Bible and says a prayer. Surrounded by family, listening to Granny's gentle voice, I'm a happy soul with a belly full of stolen bananas.

Finally, Aunty calls out that dinner is served. The smell of freshly fried fish fills the air. Nice!

I wonder if there will also be some fluffy omelettes like the ones I used to eat from the Church mess in Calcutta. Maybe I'll get lucky.

We have all sorts of delicious dishes like fish fry, spicy fish curry, and prawn curry. Yum! But you know what's missing? Omelettes!

After stuffing ourselves, everyone starts getting super sleepy. One by one, everyone goes off to their cozy bedrooms.

We cousins, we got to sleep on these squishy cotton mattresses spread out on the floor. Guess where we ended up? In Uncle's room, with his wooden desk full of boring account books.

And as I dream of jumping dolphins and flying ice creams, a grumpy monster attacks my stomach, and sleep becomes impossible.

## Passage 9: Aims, Dreams, And Aspirations

Hoping for the best!

I wake up all of a sudden, sweating and wide-eyed. Where am I? How did I get here?

The grandfather clock's TICK-tock, TICK-tock fills the room.

Oh, I remember now, I'm in Granny's home!

I sit up on the mattress. And the rumble and funny noises of the grumpy monster in my tummy are loud enough to wake up the whole house. But everyone is still sleeping, except for the noisy grandfather clock.

Ouch! My tummy hurts a lot.

I gently poke my cousin on the shoulder. I try again, a little harder this time. Finally, he wakes up with eyes as big as balloons.

"I don't feel well," I tell him.

In no time, Granny magically appears from the next room.

She soothes and calms me, leading the way to the kitchen with the dogs following, keeping their sneaky distance.

After a few minutes, a plate with small slices of raw papaya arrives.

I chomp on them slowly. They aren't sweet, but they don't taste bad either.

Granny's super-duper magic touch saves me. Soon, I fall asleep feeling much better.

The next morning, Mummy smiles at me. She's surprised that my tummy was upset. I'm not. Neither is my cousin.

Thank God, our secret attic adventure stays hidden from everyone.

***

Later in the day, Mummy says Daddy found us a new house in Ernakulam. We are going there soon.

Wow! I'm going to a new school. And I can't wait to buy books, a school bag, and make lots of new friends.

***

But things don't go exactly as we planned. Most schools don't have any more openings for new students.

Finally, we manage admission to the SRV School. It is a good school, but the classes are in Malayalam, not English.

I can already speak Malayalam. But I must now learn to read and write in Malayalam too.

So, Mummy gets me some storybooks in Malayalam.

Reading them isn't too bad, but I must put my English storybooks aside for now. I have to focus on learning Malayalam first.

My new house in Ernakulam isn't far from my school.

I make new friends. And just as I'm beginning to feel like a local Malayali, Mummy brings back my old storybooks in English along with some super-duper new ones. And our evenings are back to the fun world of stories and poems.

Now I'm getting better at juggling between two languages. In the mornings, I embrace Malayalam with its wacky words and funny sayings from school. And in the evenings, I speak proper English. It's like having double the fun, right?

***

One evening, as Mummy hands me a glass of milk, she tells me we may change schools again.

"A new school?" I exclaim in wonder.

She explains that the new school is amazing, but mainly for kids whose parents work for the government. But they also accept a few smart kids who do well in special exams each year. And guess what? I have a chance to get in if I do really well in the exams.

It's called The Central School. Mummy says we don't know how the exams will be or what the questions will be. And all I need to do is keep practising my reading and writing and hope for the best.

She explains that it will be God who will decide if I should get in or not. Well, that makes perfect sense, as always when Mummy says it.

***

I don't get to see Daddy much now.

He goes to his shop before I leave for School and comes back only when I am already snuggled up in bed. Sometimes he leaves on Sundays too. And Mummy says he is working hard to grow his new business.

I understand what it is like to be dedicated. Because my commitment to collecting his empty Berkeley cigarette packets is going strong. The stack is getting so big, it's now taking over the entire windowsill.

***

On our way back from School one day, Mummy says that the entrance exams to the new school are the next day. There's nothing to worry about. Daddy and Mummy will take me there. All I have to do is answer the questions well.

***

The next morning, we all hop into Daddy's cool car with the number plate KLA 320.

Daddy drives well, but he doesn't overtake as many cars as I want him to.

When I grow up, I'm going to drive this car super-fast because I already know everything about gears, steering wheels, accelerators, and brakes. I can't wait to be a big kid!

But first things first, I need to pass this special exam.

So we arrive at this gigantic hall. I'm sure this is the biggest hall in the whole world.

Wow! So many kids. And so many parents. And everyone looks serious.

And now I'm starting to feel a bit scared.

But you know what? Mummy knows me so well! She gives me her biggest, warmest hug and reminds me that I'm the smartest boy and I can do it. She says that she'll get me a cup of my favourite Joy Ice cream as soon as we are done with these exams.

Just hearing the word "ice cream" makes me feel better already.

I start thinking of the ice creams we used to have in Calcutta.

Daddy had taken us to this place called Flurys on Park Street. The ice cream there was really yummy—cold, creamy, and served in tall glasses that made me feel like I was in a movie. I still remember the taste, even now. We went there only once, but somehow, I can't forget how special it felt.

Joy Ice Cream is nice too. But Flurys was something else.

Then a bell rings, and Mummy and the other parents leave the hall.

The girl sitting next to me gives me a friendly smile, and I smile back. But wait! Mummy told me not to look around or talk to anyone. Oops! I'd better listen to her. I have to focus on the exams and only listen to the supervisors.

After going through all the exams one by one, I walk out of the hall feeling like a sleepy zombie with the rest of the kids.

I slump into Mummy's hug while she eyes me anxiously to see how I feel.

All I can think is that I need that ice cream right now.

## PASSAGE 10: YOU WIN SOME, YOU LOSE SOME

Journey of Triumph Leads to Barefooted Bliss.

Oh boy, waiting for the entrance exam results is like waiting for ice cream on the hottest day ever!

I've done my best in the exams. All for Mummy. She has taken so much effort to get me ready for the exams. And I want her to be happy. Always.

Finally, the big day arrives. Daddy goes to the school to check the Notice Board, and we anxiously wait for him to come back.

Right from when he opens the gate, Daddy has the biggest grin on his face. "You did it, son! Your name is on the list!" he calls out.

And I can't stop jumping around like a kangaroo. I am one of the chosen three to get into 2nd Standard! Woohoo!

Mummy and Daddy are so happy.

The sparkle in their eyes and the pride on their faces convince me that these are the happiest moments we've ever had since we came from Calcutta.

We share the good news with everyone, but there is one special person we have to tell in person—Granny.

The problem is, we can't just give her a call. Thiruvarppu doesn't have these fancy phone lines yet.

***

So, off we go on the weekend to Kottayam to share the amazing news with Granny.

We pack our bags and set off on Daddy's KLA320.

Zooming through the winding roads, we are halfway there, and suddenly, **BANG**! We come to a screeching halt.

Oh no, not again! It seems like getting a flat tyre is a tradition on every trip we take. I'm starting to think the tyres have a secret plan to annoy Daddy.

But Daddy is a superhero when it comes to changing tyres.

While he's busy doing his tyre-changing magic, I feel a rumble in my tummy.

Uh-oh, nature is calling!

Mummy asks me if I can hold it a little longer, but I surely can't. So off we race to the nearest little house on the roadside.

A lady from the house appears with a smile. Phew, relief is in sight!

As I step inside, I notice some footwear near the entrance. Being a polite little guy, I take off my rubber slippers and leave them there, catching a quick glimpse of approval on Mummy's smiling face.

While I'm in the toilet, I keep hearing strange sounds. So I look down. And oh boy, pigs are snorting up at me through the hole!

Can you believe it?

I shriek with fright, and the pigs' snorts sound scarier than a lion's roar.

I complete my mission in record time and fly out of the toilet like a scared goose.

Daddy has already changed the tyre, and soon we are on our way to Kottayam.

And just as I catch my breath, I realise something.

Oh my God! I've left my slippers outside the house. Oh, my beautiful Blue coloured Bata slippers.

I plead with Daddy to turn back. But Daddy says we'll pick up the slippers on our way back.

Mummy is the best person to get Daddy to do things. So I try my puppy-eyes look with Mummy. But that too doesn't work.

Barefooted and sulky, I sit swaying to the twists and turns of the road.

But Mummy gives me a little nudge and reminds me that nothing should dampen my spirits now.

Mummy is right, as always. So I focus my attention on the road and the way Daddy is shifting gears and handling the steering wheel.

I'm always willing and ready to help steer the car. So Daddy lets me hold my side of the steering wheel. And I'm back to being joyful and excited.

We're just about to reach where Granny's country boat always waits for us.

So I quietly tap my barefoot while practising the boat song that PappachanChettan, our boatman with big muscles, had taught me on our last visit – *"Oh dhithi thaaraa dhithithay, dhithay thaka thei thei tho"*

I'm warmed up and ready to sing it with PappachanChettan on our boat ride to Granny's home.

And this time we'll have one more thing in common. We'll both be barefoot!

## PASSAGE 11: BLOOD, SWEAT, AND GINGELLY BALLS

Slippery Saga of Family Quirks.

It feels like forever since I left my super cool slippers in that housc!

Seriously, it's been like two whole years. My hope of ever seeing them again is melting faster than my ice cream on a blazing hot day.

Daddy refuses to swing by that house and get my slippers back. He says it's not a good idea for me to go begging for my beloved footwear.

How unfair is that?

Every single time we drive past that house on our way to Kottayam, I put on a show. I cry my little heart out, scream at the top of my lungs, and even beg with all my might.

But what do Daddy and Mummy do?

They just crack up with laughter! Can you believe it?

They think it's hilarious. Daddy even says my slippers might have been eaten by the pigs in their backyard.

Sometimes, I secretly wish for a flat tyre in front of that house. At least then we'd be forced to stop, and maybe I could sneak in and rescue my dear slippers.

The ritual of getting flat tyres on every trip continues, as usual, to keep Daddy's tyre-changing skills perfect.

But no. They always happen in different places. Sigh!

Anyway, enough about my lost slippers. On the bright side, I'm doing great at my new school. Daddy and Mummy are all happy and proud because I got the 3rd rank in my 3rd-grade exams.

But Mummy is a little concerned about my health.

I tend to catch every single germ that's floating around. So she has come up with a plan to "clean" my blood.

She boils some herbs and weird dry sticks that she buys from a strange shop in the market.

While this mystery mixture is bubbling away in the pot, Mummy starts giving me a talk about the wonders of drinking this magical blend. It's supposed to purify my blood.

The boiling pot smells nasty, but Mummy promises it'll all be fine once it cools down.

Finally, she hands me a glass of that stinky drink, and I spit it out faster than you can say "yuck!" Seriously, it tastes bitter than bitter gourd!

"Son, don't sip it, just gulp it down," she says with a firm tone while handing me two gingelly balls.

So here I am, holding the most delicious treat in one hand and the most disgusting drink in the other.

I'm wondering, how can the person who loves me so much deceive me into drinking such a horrible thing? It's a total betrayal!

I feel like I'm going to vomit just thinking about taking a sip. But I gather all my courage and chug that stinky drink in one go. It's like a survival challenge.

Thankfully, those two gingelly balls are super yummy! They make everything better. Hooray for gingelly balls!

***

Mummy is serious about everything she says. Seriously, everything!

She's got rules for everything, and they're not flexible.

Like when it comes to food, there's no wasting allowed in our house. I can't take more than I can eat, and I have to finish everything on my plate. Even those little curry leaves in the curries she makes, they're meant to be eaten. Yup, every single bit!

And guess what? Yesterday, when my uncle, aunt, and cousins from Aluva came to visit, we had Upma for breakfast.

And you won't believe it, Mummy gave my cousins the same lecture about not wasting food, including those pesky curry leaves. Poor guys, they had to eat them for the first time in their lives.

The next day, when it's my turn again for the blood purification drink, I try my cutest puppy-eyes trick. But nope, she doesn't budge.

Mummy sits me down and explains again why this yucky drink is good for me. I realise there's no escape, so I just surrender and move on.

After a few days of practice, I've become a pro at chugging that horrible drink. And you know what? Those two gingelly balls are like little drops of heaven! They make everything better, seriously.

***

Saturdays are the best.

That's when my cousins in Ernakulam come over, and the whole day belongs to us.

We play tag, cricket, blindfold games, and sometimes we just run around the house until we fall on the floor laughing, too tired to move. When we've used up all our energy, we flop down beside the window in my room. That's when my favourite part begins.

The window sill in my room is wide and deep, and every Saturday, Mummy lets me fill it with water. Just enough to make a little river. That's where my snake boat lives.

It's not just any toy. Mummy got it for me during one of our trips. It's a proper replica of a real *Vallam Kali* snake boat—the kind they use in the big boat races in Kerala. Long, dark, shiny, and curved like a crescent. It even has tiny seats carved inside for the rowers.

We stand side by side at the window, leaning just enough so our hands can reach the sill outside. The water is cool to the touch, and the snake boat floats quietly, waiting.

We take turns nudging it forward with our fingers—careful not to push too hard. If it hits the edge, it might crack. Mummy says it's not like plastic toys. It's real wood. Special wood.

She's told me many times to be careful. So we are. We're not wild with this boat. We treat it like it's real.

The best part is… we don't even have to leave the room. One hand out the window, and we're in the race.

You can't play from outside though. The sill's too high. We'd need a ladder. But from inside my room, it's perfect. Like our own little river.

We push the boat gently and sing the boat song PappachanChettan taught me.

I've heard it sung loud and strong by the men from our village when they practised for the Thazhathangadi boat race—their voices booming across the water.

We try to sound like them, but we're giggling half the time.

*"Oh dhithi thaaraa dhithithay, dhithay thaka thei thei tho…"*

That's how our race begins. The boat glides. The water ripples. We cheer softly.

On Sundays, Mummy always drains the water out. She says keeping it full all the time is not good for the building. I don't argue. I just wait for Saturday to come again.

Because Saturdays are for boat races. And I always win.

***

I love my cousins so much that I never forget to remind Mummy to give them the blood-purifying drink too.

And while Mummy hands a glassful to each of them, I hand over two gingelly balls each …and explain the amazing health benefits of this wonderful drink.

They may glare at me now, but I'm sure someday they'll thank me… for keeping their blood pure and sparkling.

## PASSAGE 12: THE BIRTHDAY ALBUM

Admirals, Airplanes, and a Sister I Never Met

Birthdays are meant to be celebrated.

That's what Mummy believes.

Even though we aren't rich, my birthdays in Calcutta feel like royal events. Every year has a theme. A plan. A surprise. A little drama.

And always... a cake that matches my costume.

Once, I'm dressed as a naval admiral… and the cake is shaped like a ship.

Another year, I wear a pilot's uniform… and the cake is an airplane.

Then comes the army officer outfit… complete with a cake shaped like a military jeep.

Mummy thinks of everything.

The best part is the photos.

In every picture, I'm in character… saluting like an officer, standing like a hero. So serious, so proud. When I look at those photos, I smile. Who taught me to pose like that?

Mummy. It had to be Mummy.

She must have whispered something, maybe even tricked me into it—got me into the mood, the role, the expression. She had a way of doing that.

Everything changed after we left Calcutta.

My fifth birthday is in Ernakulam. There's no ship cake, no jeep. Instead, I'm wearing a dhoti and shirt. The caption in the photo says: "A typical Malayalee boy."

It's not grand. But somehow... it's still special.

Daddy has just started his new business. We don't have a lot. I can sense that, even if nobody says it out loud.

But Mummy doesn't let the celebration disappear. She still finds a way to make it feel like a party. That's her magic.

***

Later, when I look at the photo album, I feel like a superstar. All those costumes. All those themes. It makes me feel important. Like I was someone worth celebrating.

I have no idea how she manages to do all this.

But I can feel the excitement. I can see how special she makes the day feel.

Not just for me—but for her too.

And then... she flips to that picture.

The one where I'm barely a year old.

And I'm wearing a frock. And there's a round *bindi* on the forehead too.

"Who's this?" she asks with a mischievous smile. "This is your sister. She's in a boarding school somewhere far away."

I stare at the photo. It looks exactly like me. But in a dress.

"Mummy... this is me, right?"

She shakes her head. "No, no. That's my daughter. You haven't met her yet."

I'm confused. And slightly horrified.

I'm sure she's joking. I'm almost sure.

But the way she says it... so confident, so calm. It throws me off every time.

I don't like the idea of another child. Not one who looks like me. Not one who gets Mummy's love.

Sometimes, I believe her. Just a little. I get upset.

That's when she pulls me into a hug and says, "I'm only teasing. You're my one and only."

That hug is everything.

It makes all the confusion melt away.

Every now and then, I still go back to her with the same question—just to be sure.

She always laughs.

## PASSAGE 13: THE WAR OUTSIDE, THE CALM WITHIN

Even when war makes no sense, a mother's voice is enough

"There's a war happening," says Mummy.

I stop chewing my banana. A war? Here? In our quiet little town, where the biggest battles are over who gets the crispiest dosa? That doesn't make sense.

Mummy was talking to Daddy about it while he read the newspaper. I wasn't supposed to be listening, but I always did. Grown-up conversations were far more interesting than what they chose to tell me.

There are so many things I don't understand, but that's why Mummy exists. She always has answers. And the best part? She never gets tired of explaining, no matter how many times I ask the same thing.

So, I tug at her sari. Too many questions crowd my head, but the most important one comes out first.

"Are we going to die?"

Mummy sighs but smiles. "No, silly. We're safe."

I'm not fully convinced, but I decide to believe her. Mummy knows everything.

That evening, Daddy comes home early. That never happens. Mummy says we have to eat quickly because there might be a power cut.

Something is definitely going on.

We finish dinner, and suddenly, the night explodes with sirens.

It starts as a distant wail, stretching across the town like a long, trembling breath. Then another joins in. And another. Until the air itself is howling. The lights flicker and vanish. The darkness isn't regular night-time darkness. It's thick. Heavy. Like someone has thrown a giant black cloth over the whole town.

Mummy says we have to step outside. That's the rule.

This makes absolutely no sense.

"Shouldn't we stay inside? If something is falling from the sky, isn't a roof a good thing to have?"

Mummy shakes her head. "It's safer outside."

Safer outside? Where there's nothing between us and whatever is up there? That doesn't sound safe to me.

I stall in the verandah, leaning against our X-shaped pillar, tracing the cool, mosaic tiles with my fingers. This place is familiar, solid. This is where we always stand when Mummy brings out her camera. If anyone asks for directions to our house, we just say: Look for the one with the X-shaped pillars.

That's where I want to be. Not out there in the dark.

But Mummy calls me again, so I shuffle reluctantly to the roadside.

Neighbours are already gathered, whispering, eyes turned upward. Then—**whoosh**!

A plane. A deep, growling roar swells in the sky, louder than anything I've ever heard.

The sound is so big, it feels like it's inside my chest, shaking my ribs. I grip Mummy's fingers tightly.

My stomach twists… like when I swing too high on the swing in Kottayam and suddenly regret it.

I sneak a glance at Mummy's face. Calm. Daddy's, too.

That's how I decide we're not in real danger.

The sirens fade. The plane is gone. The town stays dark, just murmured conversations floating in the air.

For the past few days, all the car headlights have been painted with black patches. Some cars have a thick strip across the top; others, like Daddy's, just have a black dot in the centre.

This has been bothering me.

I finally ask, "Why does Daddy's car have only a black dot, but the taxi cars near Laxman Theatre have the whole top part blacked out?"

Daddy says the black dot is enough.

I'm unconvinced. So I try Mummy. "Wouldn't it look better if we did the whole top part?"

She laughs. "Then Daddy wouldn't be able to see at night."

Oh. That makes sense. The headlights of Daddy's Standard 10 are already too small.

I nod solemnly.

The sirens might be loud, the war might be confusing, but as long as Mummy keeps answering my questions, I think I'll be okay.

***

A few days pass. The sirens stop. The sky returns to being just sky.

But something inside me has changed.

I begin to realise that the world can be noisy, confusing, and full of questions — but as long as I have Mummy, I'll always find some kind of answer.

And just like that, life tiptoes back to normal.

School days tick on.

And I start hoping the holidays come soon.

## PASSAGE 14: UNCHAINED FROM VILLAGE TRADITIONS

Great Expectations – Gone With The Wind

Wow, guess what? Today is the last day of school this year! Yippee! And that means I'm going to Granny's house!

Mummy wants me to wait for a few days until Daddy is free to take us. But when Granny calls, she agrees! Mummy respects Granny's wish to have all her grandkids spend their entire holidays with her.

And I'm excited because I love the fun and freedom of being in my village.

And guess what I see when I get home?

Sunnychayan, my amazing cousin, is chatting on the porch with Mummy. He has come from Thiruvarppu to take me to Granny's. That's like a superhero rescue mission!

The Bus to Kottayam is super-fast. We're sitting in seats where we can see the road ahead. And on the way, I point to the house where I left my slippers.

Sunnychayan smiles and reminds me that those slippers would probably be too small for my growing feet now. So some other lucky kid would be wearing them, and I should be happy about it.

Oh my, I hadn't thought about it that way.

From the Kottayam Bus Stand, we take this cool bus called Vijayalakshmi to Thiruvarppu. The bus conductor and driver, and almost everyone on the bus smile at us. It's like we're famous or something!

Wow! This feels so good to be with friendly people from our village.

As we reach Thiruvarppu, I'm expecting PappachanChettan to be waiting for us in Granny's country boat. But Sunnychayan says that this time we are walking.

The first footbridge we must cross is a super-long, wobbly bridge high above the river.

Luckily, I have Sunnychayan to give me the courage to climb up the steps to the bridge.

Sunnychayan is constantly reminding me not to look down into the water.

How can I not look when there is a gap between each plank of wood that is tied together with rope?

We slowly reach the middle, and I am quite sure that the sway of the bridge is going to topple me into the water. I am catching my breath with every step I take. And my knuckles are going white while I grab the side rope.

But finally, we steady ourselves. And when the swaying of the bridge stops, we proceed to the other side. Phew!

No wonder Granny sends us the country boat every time. I had not expected so much thrill when Sunnychayan said we were walking instead of taking the boat.

Luckily, the other bridges are shorter and made of coconut tree stems. They shake a little when we walk, but Sunnychayan just ignores it like it's no big deal. And I follow.

Who needs balance when you have confidence in your elder cousin, right?

Good thing Sunnychayan is carrying my bag, so even if I fall into the water (which I didn't, by the way), my stuff will stay nice and dry.

Finally, after all that bridge-crossing excitement, we arrive at Granny's house.

And I collapse into Granny's coziest hug ever.

It makes me forget all about being tired from travelling and nervous about crossing those wooden bridges. Ah, Granny's hugs are pure magic!

At Granny's, it's always a feast for our tummies! So much delicious food, yummy snacks, and lots of fruits.

No strict timings. We eat whenever we want, and that's the best kind of freedom. And no stinky and bitter blood purification drink like Mummy makes.

***

The next morning, as usual, all of us cousins rush straight to the super-duper huge backyard behind our house.

It's like a magical kingdom full of awesome trees and open grassy lands waiting for us to explore!

We don't use the fancy grown-up toilets, oh no. We have our special spot where we do our secret morning rituals. It's our top-secret hideout! We squat a little distance away from each other. And once we finish our important business, it's time for the real adventure to begin.

We run like lightning to the sparkling streams nearby to scrub ourselves squeaky clean. It's like having our own personal spa!

My cool cousins wear waist strings (known as *Aranjaanam*) made of gold. They also wear gold chains around their necks.

Until we reach the stream, they hang their shorts onto their waist strings. Since I don't have one, I have to hold my shorts in front of me to cover myself while we run to the stream.

You see, my cousins hardly ever wear a vest or shirt, and they're always showing off their fancy gold chains on their bare chests.

And when they jump and do acrobatics in the water, they clench the dangling end of the neck chain between their lips.

It's so glamorous and exciting. How I envy my cousins!

***

So finally, after waiting for what feels like forever, Mummy and Daddy come to visit.

I can't wait to tell Mummy my important request. But, uh-oh, she doesn't seem too happy about it.

Mummy thinks that having a waist string is just a silly belief to scare away bad spirits. And she feels that gold chains are for girls, not for boys like me.

She says I should ignore the chains and waist strings my cousins wear because they're following old village customs. Since I live in a city, I need to think and behave differently.

It's a disappointment. But as always, there's something about Mummy's words that rings true and convincing.

***

On the way back to Ernakulam, Mummy and Daddy get prepared to listen to my usual cry-out to stop at the house where I left my slippers.

I'm about to tell them what Sunnychayan shared with me, and just then, I see a boy of around my age standing in front of the house.

Are those blue slippers he's wearing mine?

## Passage 15: Sugar Mountains And Flying Eggs

A Whirlwind Morning at Aunt's Place

Oh, let me tell you about the crazy breakfast time at my Aunt's place!

It's like a whirlwind, and I'm right in the middle of it all. And trying to make sense of everything that's happening around me.

I'm staying at Daddy's eldest brother's house, and it's so much fun! It's just a hop, skip, and jump away from Granny's place.

But this house, it's way more exciting than Granny's. There's always something happening here!

I am in awe of my older cousins. They're always up to something or the other. And the only confusion is, where do I look? Because all three of them get into their moods at the same time.

And there's my Aunt, the sweetest person in the whole world, trying to keep her three crazy boys happy. But let me tell you, it's like a mission impossible!

You see, something happened to my Aunt after she had her fifth child. She lost her hearing in both ears.

But that didn't stop her from living her life fully.

And she's become an expert at lip-reading! She speaks in whispers and only when it's super important.

So, here I am, sitting at this huge wooden table in the kitchen, with the most amazing aroma of hot appam in the air.

She's attending to three of her wood-fired stoves and making sure nothing gets overcooked, and adjusting the firewood so they burn according to the heat required for the cooking.

Even when sweat beads pop on her forehead, she is managing multiple tasks with skill and love. All throughout this, she is maintaining a pleasant face.

My Aunt serves me appam fresh from one of the iron pans along with vegetable stew that's simmering in a large clay pot, and it's like I'm in breakfast heaven!

But the fun is just getting started!

One of my older cousins wanders in and plunks himself down at the table. My Aunt rushes to put a plate of appam in front of him, but what does he say?

He doesn't want appam! He wants boiled eggs for breakfast.

And my Aunt already has some hard-boiled eggs ready. She puts two eggs on his plate, along with a steaming cup of black coffee.

But no, that's not enough for him!

He demands more eggs. And my Aunt tries to convince him to have a couple of appams too. But he just doesn't seem to care.

And then, another cousin walks in. He wants egg omelettes to go with his appam. My Aunt quickly places a glass of coffee with milk in front of him and starts to make those omelettes.

All the while, she's still making those delicious appams.

Soon, yet another cousin joins the breakfast battle. He wants appam and boiled eggs.

My Aunt places a steaming cup of black coffee in front of him while whipping up more appams. It's like she's a breakfast superhero, trying to fulfil all their demands.

But amid all this madness, the first cousin suddenly decides that his coffee needs more sugar.

He grabs the sugar bottle and dumps heaps of it into his cup.

I can't believe my eyes! It's like a sugar mountain in his coffee!

My head is bobbing from cousin to cousin, trying to keep up with all the action. Meanwhile, my Aunt smiles at me and serves me yet another appam. I'm so full, but they're just so tasty!

But then, things take a turn for the worse.

The third cousin, who had asked for five boiled eggs, is irritated. He's given only three, and he's not happy about it.

So he starts throwing those eggs out the window, one by one!

I sit at the edge of the wooden kitchen bench... wide-eyed, tummy full, and completely overwhelmed.

Am trying to make sense of what's happening. I've never seen anything like this before!

This? This breakfast madness would never be possible in my Mummy's presence.

She's always calm and gentle, but strict and tough.

And sure enough, the next morning… she arrives.

***

The next morning, the kitchen wasn't quite the same.

No flying eggs.

No sugar avalanches.

No cousin rolling his eyes over coffee.

Because Mummy had arrived.

She and Aunty sat together in the front room, their conversation nearly silent. Just lips moving, eyes holding emotion. I couldn't hear what they were saying.

But I can tell it's serious. Something that made the air feel different.

During breakfast, Mummy helps Aunty serve the food.

And you know what? None of my cousins are demanding more eggs or complaining about anything. They're all behaving well.

Mummy is watching them closely. The kind of watching that makes you sit straighter without even realising it.

And when one cousin reached for the sugar bottle, she gently stepped forward and asked, "Why do you need that much?"

He doesn't have an answer!

With a calm that I've only ever seen in her, Mummy continued serving breakfast. And then she spoke to all my cousins... about food, gratitude, and mothers.

Even my older cousins sat quietly, listening.

Then, once the last plate was cleared, Mummy gathered everyone, even my female cousins.

And with that same calm voice, she made an announcement.

Her medical reports had arrived.

And she must go to a place called Vellore.

For a serious operation.

Soon.

## PASSAGE 16: CAN BROKEN BISCUITS CURE BROKEN DREAMS?

A Journey of Longing

Oh, how I ache for my Mummy!

She's not here. She's in hospital in that faraway place called Vellore. Daddy is also there, taking care of her.

And my world has turned upside down.

I had to say goodbye to my school in Ernakulam and join a new school called MT Seminary in Kottayam.

School here is different from what I'm used to.

The subjects and lessons are not the same, and it's a bit hard for me. And I don't get to go home in the evening because I am in a Boarding School.

It's a lonely and discouraging life.

I look forward to Sundays the most.

Today is a Sunday, and my heart is leaping with joy and anticipation.

I'm on the first floor, scanning the distant view of the gate, waiting for that magical moment when I catch the first glimpse of my cousins who come to visit me.

And then, like a burst of sunshine, Rajuchayan's Jeep comes into view.

I hurry down the wooden steps to greet him.

And it's a joyous moment when he asks me with a caring smile – *"Enna Ondedaa?"* (which translates to a greeting similar to What's up?).

Last week, he had taken me on a short spin around the ground in his Bullet motorcycle with its engine making thunderous echoes against my School's walls.

Rajuchayan steps out of the Jeep. And we spend a few minutes talking.

Then out comes the big tin.

Every week I get a tin like this one.

It's filled to the brim with broken biscuits from Sweet House, the bakery run by Rajuchayan and Sunnychayan.

Since only the undamaged biscuits are sold to customers, the Bakery always separates the broken biscuits into tins.

This assortment of biscuits is yummy. Who cares if they are broken?

I love them so much, I'd happily eat just these for breakfast, lunch, and dinner - especially when I think about the food in our mess hall.

Some of the older boys shared this secret with us.

The meat served there is dog meat.

Once a week, a few stray dogs roaming around are caught and cooked. And the plastic mugs for serving buttermilk? They're used in the toilets after lunchtime.

Now, my friend John and I don't eat meat and avoid buttermilk.

I miss Mummy's tasty curries. How wonderful it would be if I could have even just a little bit of rice and curry cooked by her. I even miss the bitter drink she makes for blood purification. And those yummy gingelly balls.

I feel so deprived and unable to adjust to this new environment. And I don't have many friends except on Sundays.

On Sundays, I am the most popular guy because I share my biscuits with every boy in my dormitory. Only the fancy cream ones are reserved for John and me.

Though I had promised my seniors that I wouldn't tell anyone, I mention the dog's meat and plastic mugs to Rajuchayan. But he laughs loudly and says that it is nonsense.

So I try to convince Sunnychayan when he comes. But he too doesn't take it seriously.

Why don't they believe me?

I need every excuse I can get to flee from this place. All I want is to go back to my old school and my Mummy.

***

Then one day, Daddy comes to visit.

I clutch his hand while he enquires about life in the new school.

I dare not loosen my grip as I cannot afford to let go of him. I am desperately wanting him to take me to Mummy.

He says Mummy is fine and that she has sent a letter for me.

I strain to read the letter through the tears welling up in my smarting eyes.

Reading the letter, I can't stop crying.

Amidst the sobbing, I declare to Daddy that I am coming with him to Vellore. I really must see Mummy, even if it is just for a day.

Seeing that I am adamant, he takes me to the School Principal.

He wants to know why I wish to leave the school.

So I blurt out about the dog meat and the buttermilk mugs.

The senior boys are summoned. They apologetically explain that they were just kidding. It was just a prank.

But I'm just not willing to let go of either my beliefs about the food or my father's hand.

After talking for a long time, Daddy and the Principal finally made me agree to stay. They say that if I ever encounter a serious problem, I will be allowed to leave for good.

So I stand with my friend at the school gate, numb and still, as Daddy disappears into the distance.

I feel defeated and let down. My friend's hands seem more reliable than my Dad's.

At bedtime, I cry into my pillow silently until I fall into a tired slumber.

Mummy's letter is still clenched in my fist.

## PASSAGE 17: INK FROM THE HEART

A Son's Journey through a Torn Letter

A letter for me?

Really?! My heart races with excitement when a friend informs me and quickly rushes off.

My friend John looks as surprised as I am. We have never received any letters by post before.

All of us are in a hurry to get ready for the NCC (National Cadet Corps) parade practice march for the upcoming Independence Day.

We dash downstairs, wondering who could have sent me this letter.

Finally, I spot it—a blue inland letter with my name and address neatly written on it.

I wait in anticipation as the warden opens the glass shutter of the notice board displaying the letters. He smiles as he places the letter in my hands.

It's from Mummy, and I want to tear it open right away, but John says there's no time to read it now.

So we rush back to our dormitory, aware that we have only a few precious minutes to get ready for the parade. As I dress in my khaki uniform, I can't help staring at Mummy's handwriting on the letter.

What could Mummy have written? Is she doing okay? Is she coming back soon? Did Daddy tell her about the dog meat and the buttermilk mugs?

I am full of questions and anxiety as I join the other boys on the school grounds.

Excitement fills the air as boys from different classes gather in three lines, waiting for the commanding officer's signal to begin our march.

The sound of drums echoes through the atmosphere, setting the rhythm for our synchronised movements. With each beat, our feet hit the ground in perfect harmony.

Everything is beating in rhythm except my heart.

I feel restless and uneasy with Mummy's letter in my pocket.

We reach the parade ground and I can't wait any longer.

Maybe, just maybe, I can steal a few moments to read Mummy's words. After all, with so many cadets around, who would notice?

I excitedly slip my finger into the gap of the letter while looking around cautiously.

As I slit open the letter, there is something odd about it.

The letter is torn into four uneven pieces. Oh my! I have cut it open in the wrong place. What a mess!

John grips my trembling hand as I panic to salvage the muddled pieces.

And just then, our commanding officer calls out - **"Forwaaard... March!"**

So, I carefully place the torn remnants of the letter into my pocket.

The weight of my mistake is pressing upon me, and I want to scream out loud in frustration.

***

Back in school, I read the incomplete sentences in the pieces of the letter and struggle with the burden of guilt. How did I end up tearing up the letter like this?

At that moment, John becomes my lifeline, extending a hand of compassion to rescue me from the depths of despair.

Together, we painstakingly gather the jumbled pieces, like delicate petals of a broken flower.

Each piece represents my mother's love, her unwavering strength in the face of illness. With every correct alignment, our hope turns into reality.

In her delicate handwriting, I sense a shiver, a vulnerable tremor. Mummy's handwriting had always been neat and perfect.

It strikes me deeply, for it's a testament to her battle against a formidable foe. She fights not just for herself but for me, her cherished child. The letter unfolds her journey, her struggles, and her unwavering determination to heal.

Amidst her suffering, Mummy asks about my well-being, health, and studies. Her concern wraps around me like a warm embrace, momentarily easing the ache of her absence.

In those brief moments, I hold dear the special connection between Mummy and me, even when forced apart by situations we can't change.

Within the lines of her letter, a beam of light shines upon my friend John.

Mummy recognises the significance of his presence in my life, expressing gratitude for the friendship we share. It's as if my friend's spirit dances blissfully within the inked words, his importance affirmed by a mother's tender acknowledgement.

I carefully fold the letter and hold it close to my chest. The emotions within me are too overwhelming to contain. And tears continue to stream down my cheeks.

I yearn to be by my mother's side, providing comfort and happiness. Yet all I possess are her cherished words, engraved in my heart with ink as serene as the sky-blue hue of an inland letter.

My heart is heavy, but my hope is strong. I must persist in my struggle to escape from my present misery into the warmth of Mummy's embrace.

## PASSAGE 18: NOTHING FEELS THE SAME ANYMORE

Everywhere I go, leads me to wherever I don't want to go.

Looking out the window is so nice. It's like a magical world right before my eyes!

The last time I went on a train was when we left Calcutta for good and travelled to Ernakulam. It was such a memorable journey.

Daddy says we're almost at Katpadi station. From there, we'll go by road to the hospital in Vellore.

I'm feeling excited and nervous. I can't help but wonder how Mummy is doing.

Is she feeling better? What will she ask me when I see her? How long can I stay with her? There's so much I want to tell her about my school and all the things happening around me.

As the taxi stops, I want to rush straight to Mummy, but Daddy insists we put our bags in our room first.

We can't stay in Mummy's room at the hospital. Instead, we have to stay in a nearby building. We drop off our bags in our room and hurry to see Mummy.

***

Walking down the corridor, my heart beats faster and faster. I'm longing for Mummy's smile and a warm hug.

At the entrance to the room, a nurse asks us to wait outside.

I feel a bit impatient. Daddy tells me that Mummy needs some time to freshen up every day. It's part of her routine.

Finally, the door opens! Now we can go inside.

Mummy is sitting up against a big pillow.

I approach her slowly, surprising myself with my slowness. Deep down, I want to run into her arms, but there's something inside my head urging me to take it slow.

I reach out and gently hold Mummy's hand.

It feels delicate yet strong, like a lifeline connecting us in a world that feels unfamiliar and uncertain.

Mummy introduces me to the nurses as they leave the room. They smile at me with such kindness in their eyes. There's this incredible feeling of love and affection in the air.

But Mummy can't leave her bed. She has to stay there, and she gets tired very fast. This isn't the Mummy I know, full of energy and drive.

I want to share so much with her, but I don't know where to begin. There's so much to catch up on. We haven't seen each other for such a long time.

I have all these questions swirling in my mind. I don't have any answers.

Yet her loving smile is a balm to my anxious heart, assuring me that despite our separation, we are in this together.

***

Soon, it's time for Mummy to eat, and Daddy suggests we go to the canteen while she has her food in the room.

Food! Yes, that's interesting at any time.

Just that I hadn't realised while spending time with Mummy that I was getting so hungry.

I walk beside Daddy to the canteen, and the entrance looks different from regular restaurants.

Instead of steps, there's a sloping floor that leads up toward the entrance. And around it, there are steel railings.

The canteen is very neat. The silvery steel furniture and the food counter are gleaming clean.

And the food is very tasty, especially when compared to the food I get in the boarding school mess.

***

So now, when I am not spending time with Mummy, there's only one place I want to be – the canteen.

Almost always, the canteen is empty. That is, except for this boy I see there all the time. He looks like he's my age but has golden yellow hair. The thing is, he is always doing acrobatics on the steel railings.

After a long wait, I approach him when he pauses his twists and turns.

Although we talk in English, his words are different and longer. And he speaks in a funny tune. Even so, we become friends. Just that he is constantly swinging and dangling from the steel railings.

He is not from India. Just like me, his mother is here for treatment.

Occasionally, his Father and elder sister with the same golden yellow hair come to the canteen and talk to him, but he's always too busy with his acrobatic circus.

I secretly try to imitate his acrobatics, but I soon realise it's not easy. He's amazing! How does he do it?

Every day, I spend more time with my friend in the canteen than with Mummy. She rests most of the time, and there are always nurses and doctors in her room when she's awake.

But every day, I get to sit beside Mummy and talk to her. She tells me that Daddy is arranging for me to go back to my old school in Ernakulam.

Wow! I always knew I could convince Mummy about leaving boarding school.

"So, when are you coming home?" I ask her eagerly.

Mummy says she'll come home soon, but for now, she has to stay in the hospital. So, I'll be staying with a family friend in Ernakulam.

Now I'm confused.

Should I be happy? Going back to my old school is wonderful, but the main reason I want to return is to be with Mummy. Otherwise, what's the point?

Unanswered questions and thoughts swirl in my mind, but at least I have something good to share with my friend tomorrow at the canteen.

Although I can't physically perform his acrobatics, my thoughts and emotions dangle and twist more vigorously than he ever could.

## PASSAGE 19: DOODLER ON THE ROOF

How to be a perpetual nuisance

One more round, please. I beg Rajuchayan.

I love Rajuchayan's Bullet motorcycle. The distinct thump of the engine reverberates with power, giving me a blood rush that I can't get enough of.

It's my last Sunday at MT Seminary School, Kottayam. And sadly, the final visit from my cousins Rajuchayan and Sunnychayan.

Shifting to the Ernakulam school means I'll miss them dearly, along with the precious tin of broken biscuits from their bakery, my weekly delight.

In just a couple of days, Daddy will arrive to take me back to my old school in Ernakulam. I am excited as I pack my bags. And I eagerly await his arrival.

Finally, Daddy arrives.

***

After completing the necessary paperwork, we load my bags into the dicky of KLA320 – Daddy's wonder car.

I can see that Daddy has the spare tyre ready to be rolled into action any time we have our usual tyre puncture on our trips.

I'm thrilled that Daddy has arranged for my re-admission to my old school. Central School, here I come!

As we approach home, a sense of warmth envelops me, but it quickly fades as I step inside.

The house is in disarray and neglect. Mummy's little garden has been reduced to dried stubs and anthills. Hardy weeds stubbornly emerge from the cracks in the stone pathway.

The rooms have collected dust and wear a gloomy look as if silently protesting against Mummy's absence.

***

Tomorrow, Daddy will drop me off at Sally Aunty's house, where I'll stay until Mummy comes back from the Hospital.

Everything has been happening so fast that I couldn't ask Daddy enough questions about what to expect in this new place.

But as soon as I meet Sally Aunty, she welcomes me with motherly love and care, instantly making me feel comfortable. Her loving embrace soothes my worries and makes me feel at home.

Returning to my old school feels like stepping into a cherished dream. The laughter of friends and familiar faces surrounds me.

However, there's no time to relax as the final exams are approaching.

***

One day, my class teacher calls me aside. She knows I had gone to Vellore to meet Mummy and lovingly asks how she is.

Then comes the news I didn't want to hear – I won't be promoted to the 6th grade.

I look at her like I've been struck by lightning.

So she explains that I studied different books in my previous school, and I won't be able to perform satisfactorily in the exams here.

I feel like my world is crumbling. Why didn't anyone warn me about this academic ambush?

The two main reasons why I wanted to come to Ernakulam were to be with Mummy and to be back with my friends at my school.

But look where I stand now.

Mummy is still in Vellore, and my friends are going to leave me behind in my class while they progress on to the next grade.

I struggle to let these realities sink into my head. Couldn't I have just remained in my old school?

Thankfully, my teacher gives me a couple of minutes to regain my composure. I must resolve that even when I fail in my exams, I will not let this setback defeat my courage.

Who needs the 6th grade when I can have a tribe of friends from both the 5th and 6th grades? Double the friendship, double the fun. How about that!

***

I become one of the tallest in my class and naturally gravitate to the back bench. And let me tell you, the back bench is the best place to be!

From here, I have a helicopter view of the entire class, fewer disturbances from teachers, and more fun with my classmates.

Plus, my doodling skills improve. Now, a whole lot of the back pages of my notebooks transform into canvases for caricatures of guitarists and drummers and the Woodstock logo (small bird perched on a guitar neck) and different adaptations of the peace logo.

Back home, I don't have to worry about Mummy checking my books, so I let my imagination run wild on the pages. Caricaturing western music stars becomes my obsession, even if I don't have any cassettes of that kind of music.

All my caricatures wear bell-bottom trousers and flowery shirts. And they boldly flaunt Woodstock logo amulets and lockets on their beaded necklaces.

The bass drum of the jazz drum set in my caricatures often has the Woodstock logo or some groovy names, which we friends mutually agree are suitable for a band.

During breaks between classes, my classmates gather around and enjoy my caricature skills. And their encouragement motivates me even more. I'm loving every bit of this artistic journey!

Some of my classmates make paper aeroplanes and rockets, or paper fortune tellers and go around the class revealing handwritten fortunes inside them.

But hey, I can't waste a single page. My doodles are taking over, and I need all the space I can get.

It's incredible how my self-taught, imaginative doodling soars higher than any paper aeroplane. And I don't need a fortune-telling game to afford me a glimpse into an imaginary future.

I'm already living in the unknown, and learning that each twist and turn leads me to unexpected destinations irrespective of what I hope for.

Oh, and you know what I'm secretly hoping for? That none of my teachers catch wind of my doodle empire. I can't bear the thought of them inspecting my notebooks in detail and hitting the proverbial roof.

Because when the world feels too messy to make sense of, doodling is how I quietly fight back — one wild hairstyle and bell-bottom at a time.

## PASSAGE 20: SO CLOSE, SO FAR AWAY

When good times end much too soon

Finally, Mummy returns.

But the sight of Mummy now is very different from the last time I saw her in Vellore.

She can no longer walk and has to be carried around. Her head is covered with a scarf. Her once flowing curly hair is gone, and her entire left hand is tightly bandaged. And she looks frail.

Looking at Mummy's head makes me uncomfortable and a little scared.

The stitches from her operation have left a long scar on her scalp, and the area around it looks slightly dented.

Sometimes, a Doctor comes to visit her, and I try to catch glimpses through the curtains to see what's happening inside her room. The Doctor takes out a small steel hammer and knocks on her left knee, but Mummy remains seated as if nothing happened.

I gradually understand that the muscles on the left side of her body have become very weak.

***

Then, one day, Daddy tells me that we are moving to another house, closer to my school.

As the moving day arrives, our belongings are shifted, and the house starts to feel empty.

It has been raining since morning.

The sound of the thrashing rain echoes through the empty house. And the sombre atmosphere seems to reflect the painful helplessness of Mummy.

Finally, the rain reduces to a slight drizzle. And it's time to take Mummy to the car.

Mummy appears relaxed as she reclines in the big cane chair while being carried to the car... the same chair that once made her look regal and at ease.

But now, two men carry her in it, slowly, carefully, across the front yard. Someone walks beside her, holding a large black umbrella to keep her dry.

Everyone seems a little annoyed by the rain, but there's a faint lopsided smile on her face as if she's finding relief in the tiny raindrops falling on her.

And I don't know why... but something about that smile makes me feel a little sad.

Maybe she doesn't care about getting wet anymore.

Maybe the rain feels soft compared to all the other things she's been going through.

It's bittersweet to see her like this – strong in spirit, but weakened by her illness.

***

The new house is lovely.

It has big windows, clean white walls, and a gate with a bright green latch.

In the mornings, I swing the gate open and walk to school by myself, pretending I'm an office-going uncle. I reach just in time, never early, never late... and that feels so nice.

After school, I don't have to rush home like before. I can stay back a little longer to play volleyball with my friends.

When I finally return, I'm allowed a few minutes with Mummy in her room.

She especially enjoys listening to me singing the prayer song I learned from my boarding school in Kottayam.

There at the boarding school, I used to sing this song every evening along with the rest of the children, without much thought or feeling.

But back home, when I sing it softly in Mummy's room, her eyes always light up.

Only now am I beginning to feel the beauty of its words.

"മഴവില്ലും സൂര്യചന്ദ്രനും

വിണ്ണിലെ പൊന്നിൻ താരകളും

യേശുവിൻ കൃപകളെ വർണ്ണിയ്ക്കുമ്പോൾ

പാടും... ഞാനുമത്യുച്ചത്തിൽ"

("The rainbows, the sun and the moon, and all the golden stars in the sky— when they proclaim the grace of Jesus, I too will lift my voice in praise.")

***

When Mummy speaks now, her face looks uneven. One side doesn't move the way it used to. Yet her smile shines through her loving eyes.

There's a touch of pain in her smile as if it holds deeper meanings than just a casual expression. With her bald head and weary appearance, she looks like a different person.

I can see that I'm losing her gradually, as the opportunities to be with her become scarce. I yearn for those precious moments of love and care that we used to share.

Whenever I peek into her room, someone says, "Not now."

It's either medicine time. Or sponge bath time. Or time for her to rest.

Sometimes, it's the bedpan.

I understand. But I still miss her.

***

One day, I walk into her room, not realising that she is being given a sponge bath.

Seeing Mummy's partially naked body, I stop abruptly in my tracks. And I quickly leave the room feeling a sense of guilt.

I can't bear the thought of her struggling to maintain her privacy and dignity while her illness exposes her body to others.

Now I am cautious and hesitant about visiting her room. I wait until someone tells me I can go in. Sometimes I don't go in at all.

It feels like she needs solitude. And I fear that my presence might burden her further.

In the depths of my heart, I long for my vibrant mother, the one with flowing curly hair, an unstoppable zest for life, and an aura radiating strength.

The woman in the next room looks and feels like a stranger.

***

And just when I think I couldn't feel more unsure…

I walk into the drawing room one evening and find two guests deep in conversation.

They're talking in low voices, but I catch my name. And Mummy's.

"...because of the pregnancy," one of them says. "So unfortunate..."

The other sighs loudly. Then silence.

They stop talking the moment they notice me. They smile politely, like nothing happened.

But something had. I'm sure of it.

I wasn't supposed to hear it, but I did. Not all of it, but just enough to confuse everything inside me.

Were they saying that I was the reason Mummy got so sick? That something about my birth caused all this pain?

I want to forget what I heard. Maybe I misheard. Maybe they didn't mean it that way.

But the words stick to me like damp clothes on a rainy day. I carry them everywhere, unsure what to do with them.

Mummy's still in her room, resting. And I don't dare ask her.

What if it's true?

What if, by just being born, I started the pain that changed her life?

I don't know.

And that not knowing makes everything harder.

***

Then, one evening, my uncle says that Mummy wants to talk to me.

My heart races as I enter her room.

I don't know what she's going to say.

But something in the air feels different... like I'm about to hear something I won't like.

And I'm not ready.

I want to go back.

Back to when her gentle voice and caring presence filled every corner of the house.

I wish I could fix everything... press a magic button and bring her old self back.

But I don't even know what to say when I walk in.

All I know is… this moment feels like the end of something.

And I'm not ready for more bad news.

## PASSAGE 21: THE SHADOW IS CAST

Can you replace the irreplaceable?

There is no one else in the room.

As I walk into Mummy's room, this is the first thought that comes to my mind. I don't remember having Mummy all to myself in a room ever since she returned from the Hospital.

Mummy is sitting up on the bed, propped against a pillow. She is sitting facing the entrance of the room. And our eyes meet as I walk in.

Mummy seems less tired today. And I can't take my eyes off her gaze.

I can sense a range of emotions flashing through her expressive eyes.

I wonder why Mummy asked for me. What does she want to talk about?

She looks relaxed and prepared to welcome me. Yet I walk towards her with caution and measured steps. I have a feeling that even my footsteps are to be appropriately placed on the floor of this room.

I stand nervously, fidgeting with the chair that's placed next to her bed.

Mummy senses my hesitation and smiles warmly. She gestures to me with her right hand to come near. So I pull the chair closer to her bed.

But before I can sit, she gestures to me to sit beside her on her bed. I have to be careful not to hurt her left hand, which is tightly bandaged.

Mummy then waits for me to settle down and get comfortably seated next to her.

She runs the fingers of her right hand through my hair fondly. And I sit with my eyes shut, quietly relishing the joyful moment. I am being transported back to when Mummy was healthy and life was wonderful.

It's been so much time since I have received such attention and care from her.

***

Mummy breaks the silence and asks how I am doing. How's school? How are studies? How are my friends?

I promptly give her a rosy picture of everything, hoping she will not ask to see my notebooks. It's going to be quite a task to explain all those pages of doodling.

Fortunately, she has something else on her mind.

Mummy says there is something in particular that she wants me to understand. Her expressions give me no clue as to what she wishes to say, but I suspect it's something serious.

As I sit in attention to listen, Mummy says that she will not be living much longer. She says she is going to die soon.

I can't believe what I'm hearing.

I sit speechless. My world is collapsing into a blur.

I must have looked at her with an expression of blankness because she slowly repeated her words.

How can this be? I wonder. Is there no way the doctors can save my Mummy?

While I struggle in confusion and helplessness, Mummy pulls me gently towards her and kisses me on my forehead and both my cheeks. And I burst out in grief.

Mummy says that she expects me to be brave. And that I must be strong enough to understand and accept that I would soon have to live without her.

I can barely hear her words between my uncontrollable sobs.

I want to be brave. As brave as Mummy expects me to be.

And I want to measure up to the courage Mummy displays.

Yet, my grief is getting the better of me. And I don't even dare to look at Mummy's face now.

I don't want to see her cry.

Mummy holds me against her chest and raises my lowered face, and continues talking.

And I am surprised how she can continue to keep a loving smile on her face even when sharing such terrible news.

Mummy explains that Daddy is still young. So he will be marrying again and bringing me a new mother. And this new mother would take good care of me.

She emphasises that she has already met her, and this new mother is a good woman and would love me as much as Mummy loves me. She affirms that I would be very happy with her.

I don't understand how I can ever be happy without Mummy in my life.

But I'm too shocked to react.

Mummy wants me to promise that I will always be good to my new mother and obey her at all times.

So I obediently nod my head in acceptance while continuing to weep silently.

Mummy waits patiently for me to get a grip on myself. And all through this, Mummy maintains her composure.

It's as though she has thought this out well and has prepared her mind to strengthen me. Throughout our conversation, not even for a moment does Mummy falter in her confidence and clarity.

***

We must have sat silently for quite a while. And I am struggling to keep myself from sobbing. Inside, I feel like screaming out my resentment at the injustice that's thrust upon me.

Then, after giving me one more hug, Mummy says she is tired and will talk to me later.

All of a sudden, she seems exhausted and in need of rest. I can see that she needs to be left alone.

As I get down from the bed and walk out of the room, Mummy reminds me to be brave.

"Yes, I will be brave", I say while wiping the tears burning down my cheeks.

## PASSAGE 22: MY HEART WILL GO ON

Didn't get to say goodbye

I'm so happy.

Our house is full of guests. Uncles, aunts, cousins, and friends whom I don't often get to meet.

I enjoy the attention and love. And I feel special.

Everyone is talking and catching up in the drawing room.

Even though my room is small, I squeeze in with my cousins and friends. And we huddle together, chatting.

Suddenly, there's a hush.

I look into the drawing room and see our priest. I quietly go up to him and stand beside his chair. He asks how I'm doing, and I answer, feeling a little nervous.

Just then, my elder cousin Babuchayan arrives from Kottayam. I take him to see Mummy.

As we enter Mummy's room, we see that Mummy is having trouble with something in her mouth.

Usually, Uncle Kochunny is always around to supervise things. When Uncle is around, everything goes smoothly. But right now he is in the drawing room talking to the priest.

I look for the lady who helps Mummy. But before she can come, Babuchayan helps Mummy. He cleans something that comes out of her mouth without hesitation and goes to wash his hands.

I can't believe what I'm seeing. The last time Babuchayan and Mummy met was long back in Kottayam.

She had scolded him along with his brothers for having too many eggs for breakfast, and for dumping heaps of sugar into their tumblers of coffee. But now, he's helping her so gently.

Babuchayan returns from the bathroom. And I can see that he is glad for the opportunity to help Mummy.

In a moment, the priest comes in, and we all assemble to pray.

While we pray, Mummy opens her eyes a little. She's been tired and sleeping a lot lately. But now her eyes are focused on the priest. She is always serious about prayers.

After the prayer, Daddy wipes Mummy's lips with a cloth dipped in a small bowl of water. He then hands it over to me. I wonder why. Mummy doesn't seem to be drinking the water. But then I simply obey.

Later, we return to the drawing room. And soon, the priest and a few people leave. So it's time for us cousins and friends to come back to my room to chat. We don't often have the opportunity to see each other, so it's a special occasion.

By late evening, everyone leaves. And I am back to being alone.

***

The next day, too, we have a few relatives and guests visiting Mummy. But I'm feeling dull because there are no kids around.

I've not been going to School for the past couple of days. And I am missing my friends.

I sit reading a book. But I'm feeling disappointed.

It's already the 4th day of December. And I can see many of the neighbouring houses twinkling with lights, stars hung proudly at their doors, much ahead of Christmas.

I've asked Daddy and Uncle Kochunny if we can hang a star at our entrance too, but they're always busy.

I sigh and turn a page, trying to focus.

And then, a bell rings.

Sharp. Sudden.

Not a gentle chime. Not a polite call.

It's the bell that's kept beside Mummy's bed.

It rings again. And again. And again.

Loud. Continuous.

Urgent.

The sound slices through the house like a siren.

I've always liked that bell, even though I got in trouble for playing with it before.

I know Mummy uses it to ask for help. But she never rings it like this. Not this long. Not this desperate.

I jump up. My feet move before my thoughts can catch up.

We all rush to her room.

But it's not Mummy ringing the bell. It's Uncle Kochunny. And it's ringing so shrilly that it seems to scream more than call.

And I'm confused.

Mummy's eyes are wide open. Too wide.

And her eyeballs are rolling upward... showing more white than I've ever seen.

Her mouth is frozen open, and her chin lifts in small, jerky gasps. She is struggling for breath.

Daddy's grip on my hand is so tight. I want to tell Daddy that he's hurting me. But I am not able to take my eyes off Mummy's face.

In all the confusion, I see that Mummy has stopped struggling.

Her eyes are still wide open. And now her entire eyes are white. The eyeballs have disappeared.

Uncle steps forward, his movements tender and final. He gently closes her eyes.

Mummy's gone.

I hear the voices of grief all around me.

But I stand frozen... the shrill ring of the bell still in my ears.

Why didn't anyone tell me that these were Mummy's final moments?

Why didn't I get to hug her and tell her I love her?

## Passage 23: The River Knew

A Journey I Almost Forgot Was a Goodbye

Mummy's body is placed in a wooden casket.

The ambulance has come to take her to our church in Kottayam. It's about a two-hour journey from our home in Ernakulam.

I stand quietly as the big white ambulance reverses into position.

Six men lift the casket from the drawing room, after the priest finishes his prayers.

I watch every step, my heart tight, scared that Mummy might fall if they aren't careful. But they carry it slowly and surely.

The ambulance door closes.

I realise I'm not going in the ambulance.

Instead, I get into a car with two of my cousins from Ernakulam. One of my uncles is driving. It's quiet inside. No one speaks much. But it doesn't feel heavy—just serious. The kind of quiet grown-ups seem to understand better than I do.

The road ahead is familiar. We always take this route to visit Granny in Thiruvarppu. I know it like a map in my head—bends, trees, potholes, shops with blue shutters.

Then comes the big, old arched bridge—Nagampadom Bridge.

I sit up straighter. I always do when we cross it. That's how I know we've reached Kottayam town.

The streets grow busier as we pass through the heart of Kottayam. Familiar shops, old movie posters, and bicycles stacked in front of tea stalls flash past the windows.

But no one in the car says a word.

Our silence feels strange… like when something's wrong, but no one wants to say it out loud.

We leave the town behind and head toward our village. The road narrows, bending past green fields and quiet houses. Soon, we reach Illickal Bridge.

It's the same bridge that always made my heart race when I was younger. It rattles with every car that goes over it—like it's been trying to collapse for years but keeps deciding not to.

Soon, the cars ahead begin to slow down.

***

We've stopped beside the river—but not at the usual spot where PappachanChettan waits to pick us up. That's odd.

We've come further ahead to a broader opening of the river.

There are bigger country boats waiting, their bamboo poles resting beside them. A few boatmen are already standing nearby. I can see the ambulance too, parked a little ahead.

This stretch is wider, calmer. The banks are gently sloped, with small houses and coconut trees lining the sides. I see people gathering in their courtyards, quietly watching. Some have walked to the edge of the water.

They stand in clusters, some barefoot, some with their hands behind their backs, murmuring softly, their gazes fixed on us.

We don't usually stop here.

The ambulance door opens, and I watch as Mummy's casket is lifted again—this time onto a large country boat. It has a wide wooden platform laid out specially for the casket.

I'm told to get in.

Daddy climbs in too, along with a few aunts and uncles. Not many of us. It feels quiet again. Respectful.

My cousins are asked to get into a different boat—a smaller one, filled with more people. They look uncertain, but they listen.

Our boat doesn't move yet.

Theirs does.

I see their boat pull away gently from the jetty. My cousins turn back and wave at me, their faces bright with excitement and a bit of pride. I wave back, but I'm not happy.

Why are we not moving?

I look at Daddy. "Why didn't we use the usual jetty where PappachanChettan comes?" I ask.

He says this place is wider. That too many boats can't gather at our regular stop. This is easier for everyone.

But I don't like it. The other boats have already started. Ours is still here. We've missed our chance to lead.

Our boat is bigger. Our boatmen are stronger. I wanted to show off a little to my cousins from Ernakulam. Show them I know this river. I know this place.

Now they'll reach first. That's not fair.

Finally, we begin to move.

The boatmen stand tall, pushing their long bamboo poles deep into the riverbed and steering us forward with slow, practiced ease. The water glides around us with gentle swirls.

The breeze lifts lightly across the deck—warm with the scent of riverbanks and faintly sweet from the wreaths and flowers placed beside Mummy's casket. A mix of jasmine, roses, and marigolds. I breathe it in without realising. It smells like love.

The boat sways gently, and my eyes wander to the ripples the bamboo poles make in the water. The sun glints off the surface, and for a moment, it feels like any other boat ride.

Without thinking, I whisper a tune under my breath.

*"Oh dhithi thaaraa dhithithay, dhithay thaka thei thei tho…"*

It's the boat song PappachanChettan taught me. I used to sing it every time we came to visit Granny. It was always fun. Always a game.

But halfway through, the words catch in my throat. I stop.

This boat ride… isn't the same.

Along the riverbank, more people are standing outside their homes. Some are leaning on fences. Some have children in their arms. Everyone watches silently as we pass.

No one waves. No one smiles.

***

We reach the church. The casket is lifted once more and carried into the cool, quiet building. The priests are waiting. The candles are lit. The prayers begin.

And that's when it hits me. I see Mummy's face again. And I remember why we're here.

We're not here for a boat ride.

We're here to say goodbye.

## PASSAGE 24: THE TWINKLE IN THE TEARS

A bad month to die

It's Christmas time. And I'm hating it.

The whole village is cheerful. But I am not.

Colourful decorations dangle outside the houses. And multi-coloured miniature lights twinkle from trees.

But at Granny's house, there's only one star, and it's sad like me.

And it hangs from the hook of the verandah's ceiling with an abandoned look.

Its glaring light attracts flies and night bugs. And the pointed tip at the bottom is collecting dead insects, making it appear dark and grim.

Christmas season is always the happiest.

But Granny says there must not be any celebrations for 40 days from when Mummy died. We will quietly celebrate the birth of Christ.

Every few days, I go with my cousins and Granny to where Mummy rests.

We make our way through the maze of graves. And clean up the remnants of burnt-out candles and wilted flowers. We light a few candles, cupping the flickering flames from the gusty breeze. And spend a few silent, prayerful moments listening to the rustling of leaves and the creaking of nearby trees.

On Sundays, we have the priest come over and do a prayer around the grave.

***

The nights during the Christmas season are filled with festive cheer. No one can stop the carollers from barging in.

Most nights, noisy groups of boys and men come holding colourful balloons and bright lanterns that smell like kerosene. We watch them clap and sing Christmas songs and hymns in Malayalam, shouting like they're trying to wake up the whole world!

Though Granny says we're not allowed to celebrate, out here, Christmas doesn't seem to care.

It's still coming. Still glowing. Still singing.

Maybe it knew I needed it to come. Just a little bit.

My cousin and I stare at Santa's baggy costume, and peek from the sides of Santa's mask and fluffy cotton beard to guess which of our neighbours has come pretending to be Santa.

Luckily, before Santa's mask starts sliding off or his cotton beard gets blown away, Granny comes out and gives them some money.

Just like that, they cheer up, and shout out "Happy Christmas!" and burst into a funny little thank-you song—as if they're saying, "Thanks for the treat, we're young and free and off to sing at the next house!"

I try not to smile… but a small one sneaks out anyway. Maybe Christmas found a way in after all.

***

There's plenty of food laid out on the dining table, but I'm not in the mood. I can only eat vegetarian dishes, while everyone else enjoys various fish and meat dishes.

Granny has explained that I am to be on a period of prayer and fasting for 40 days. This means that I can have only vegetarian food. This is our religious tradition to honour the departed soul.

I understand my Granny. But it's Christmas. And it's not fair that I can't eat what everyone else can.

It's not fun being left out.

***

After dinner, my older cousins bring out boxes of crackers. We gather a short distance from the house and light them one by one.

Granny doesn't approve. But with the freedom my older cousins demand, they do what they want.

Now and then, when I run past Granny, she reminds me to calm down.

Granny is right. I am constantly forgetting that I am supposed to be in mourning. And I feel a pang of guilt.

But as soon as I see all the lively things happening outside, I feel excited again.

***

Finally, the holiday season comes to an end. And the village is back to its normal life.

The days pass. And after the 40th-day prayers, we go to Ernakulam. Granny is coming with us.

It's a new house now. Daddy shifted to the new house while we were in Kottayam. I can't walk to School anymore. I have to take a bus and leave early.

Now Granny has become both my Mummy and my Granny. And I love it.

There is a touch of old-fashioned charm in everything Granny does. Especially in the food she cooks. And life slowly starts to feel normal again.

Every evening, she shares stories from the Bible.

I miss Mummy when it comes to getting help with my studies. And more intently in the evenings when we pray for her.

But Granny is not happy living in a city. In this small house with a small compound, she feels lonely.

She misses the freedom of her village life, where she can walk around in the big compound and take care of the cows and the hens and the ducks. So we go to Kottayam often.

I am amused at the thought that when Mummy was around, we used to go to Kottayam to be with Granny. Now, when living with Granny in Ernakulam, we go to Kottayam to ease Granny's homesickness.

***

A few months pass, and we are in Kottayam during the weekend. And I can see some serious discussion happening in the front room between Daddy and his brothers.

While I'm busy running around, my Aunty calls me aside. She sits me close to her and tells me that there's something important I need to know.

Daddy is getting married soon.

## PASSAGE 25: DON'T ROCK MY BOAT

Sailing at the mercy of the winds of change

Daddy is going to get married again?

I stare silently at Aunty's face.

She pulls me into a hug, her voice soft and careful. "Daddy is marrying again," she says gently, "so that you can have a mother to take care of you."

I blink, confused. "But I don't need a new mother," I say quickly. "I can take care of myself."

She listens quietly.

"We're okay—Daddy and me. Just the two of us. We can manage."

My words come out in a rush. I want her to understand how strongly I feel about this. I say it again, a little louder this time, as if saying it more will make it more true.

Aunty doesn't stop me. She just lets me speak.

Then, after a pause, she says gently, "Yes son, I know. But Daddy is still young. And he wants to marry again."

Her eyes are soft but steady. I can see from her sympathetic eyes that it's not easy for her to be the one who has to convey this news to me.

She pulls me closer to her.

Aunty has seen how our lives have turned upside down during Mummy's sickness and death.

And every member of the family is doing what they can to support us in this period of drastic change.

I can see that she is trying to deliver this news as gently as possible.

Aunty speaks slowly and softly, giving me enough time to understand the situation and its impact.

I just stay quiet in her arms.

Somewhere inside, I know things are changing. I just wish they weren't.

Granny is doing her best to keep things as normal as possible. That's why she even became willing to stay with us in Ernakulam to take care of me.

Now, just as things were starting to look better, this news is unsettling.

Why is it that Daddy wants to ruin the comfort of our lives when we are finally able to live peacefully?

Aunty wipes the tears rolling down my cheeks. And her loving hug is a big relief. But I simply am unable to keep myself from sobbing helplessly.

I don't want Daddy and his brothers to hear my sobs.

I lean on Aunty's shoulder. And we sit there quietly.

I know I'll start crying again if I look at Aunty's face. It's much easier to keep my head low and stare at the floor.

My cousins come running in every few minutes, all full of noise and "Come, let's play!".

But all my energy's gone.

I wipe my face quickly, pretending like I'm not crying. But I know they've seen.

They are confused. And stand beside me, wondering what is preventing me from going out to play.

But I'd rather look at the floor than anyone's face. And wish they'd stop standing there.

Aunty tells them gently to go out and play. I'll join them after some time.

They listen, but they keep glancing back at me as they leave.

My head is beginning to throb.

I hate crying. And I don't like others to see me crying.

Even though I'm trying to stop crying, my tears just won't listen.

Life is so unfair.

Can't God see?

Are we not barely surviving from the pain of losing Mummy? And are we not gradually adapting to the new reality of a world without Mummy?

Sitting here, though my eyes are blurred, I can see things now.

Mummy had told me this would happen.

She had told me that she was going to die soon and that Daddy would marry again.

And I had promised her that I would be a good son to my new Mummy.

Pushing back those words from my memory is my fault. I have always known that Mummy never said anything she didn't mean. And she had prepared me for what lay ahead.

I had wiped off those memories like they were just a bad dream. But now, they zoom back to stare me in the face.

This is reality. And I must face it like Mummy explained.

Yes, Mummy. I won't let you down.

I can see Mummy's face smiling confidently at me. And I know I must be strong and brave, as she had said.

I finally calm my mind, and I smile at Aunty to show her I'm okay with the idea.

By then, my cousins come back again. So I tell Aunty I'm going out to play.

***

Later in the evening, we leave for Ernakulam. And throughout the trip, Daddy remains quiet and lost in thought.

So I spend my time showing Granny all the places on the familiar roads.

***

The next weekend, we're back in Kottayam. And Daddy calls me aside and says we're going to meet someone in town later.

I wonder who it could be because we don't usually do any house visits after Mummy left us.

But I'll go anywhere Daddy wants me to.

***

As we enter the compound, I feel nervous.

Whose house is this? Who are we meeting? Why is Daddy making it a surprise?

We park the car, and a man is waiting for us on the porch. We go in and get seated. And a lady brings us refreshments.

Everyone is nice, but I don't know any of them. So I focus on all the interesting stuff on the plates while Daddy talks.

After a while, another lady comes in. She smiles too, as friendly as everyone else. And she joins the conversation.

In a short while, the man suggests they go to another room, leaving the new lady with me.

All this while, while cleaning up the snacks on my plate, I've been fascinated by this wonderful thing on a table at the other end of the room. I'm sure it's a music player, but with super big tape spools. And it's different from what I've ever seen before.

The new lady notices my interest and we walk over to it. I'm amazed by the spools, the switches and the buttons. And while I imagine how it would work, she asks if I know who she is.

Of course, I don't know her. But her face does seem a bit familiar.

But before I can say anything, she tells me she's going to marry Daddy and be my new Mummy.

I feel awkward and don't know where to look.

I keep smiling, but I'm confused.

The new lady keeps talking, but I can't pay attention. I just want to know where Daddy and everyone else are.

So is this the lady Mummy meant? Have I met her before?

It's all so confusing, and I don't know how to react. I keep politely smiling as she talks a bit more.

Finally, Daddy and the others come back, and it's time to leave. Soon, we get in the car and wave goodbye.

Daddy is again back in thought, and I am enjoying the pleasant breeze as we pass by the Thazhathangadi river.

And suddenly I am reminded of what PappachanChettan, our boatman, told me when I first travelled on our country boat – "Always sit safely away from the boat's edge. **You never know when your boat can get rocked."**

## PASSAGE 26: WINDS OF CHANGE

Ring Out The Old, Ring In The New

We have to visit "Jos Brothers" today evening, Daddy says during breakfast.

I am in a hurry, gobbling up fistfuls of puttu (steamed flour of ground rice layered with coconut shavings) before I run to the Bus Stop to catch a Bus to school.

Usually, nothing in the world can convince me not to stay back in school for fun. But getting new clothes from Daddy's favourite textile shop is exciting.

Granny walks in from the kitchen with more steaming hot puttu, but I must run. I can easily have one more log of Granny's tasty puttu and kadala curry (a spicy black chickpea curry). But there's no time today for more.

If I don't make it to the morning assembly on time, PT (Physical Training) Master – Xavier Sir is sure to make me stand outside.

He enjoys enforcing rules in School. And I, unfortunately, am his prized target because he and Daddy were college buddies.

The best way to keep out of trouble is to keep out of his sight, but unfortunately, his hawkish eyes can spot me from anywhere.

I make it to the assembly just in time. And stand pretending not to notice Xavier Sir's smug look that says, "That was a narrow escape this time. I almost got you."

***

Back home in the evening, I hurriedly get ready to go shopping. But convincing Granny to come along is a battle in itself. I want her by my side and manage to convince her to come.

All of us get new clothes, and I'm thrilled. Back home, I wonder when we can wear them.

Granny says, "These are for Daddy's wedding."

"Oh! When is that?" I think.

Nobody has been talking about Daddy's wedding, not even my cousins.

I haven't forgotten about it. But I don't want those thoughts to come up. Maybe it would fade away on its own, like a bad dream.

But why do my nightmares keep coming back?

I am a bit worried at bedtime. Because on some mornings, I find my bed wet.

It doesn't happen often, but the fear that it can happen haunts my thoughts.

I used to be the proud bedkeeper when Mummy was around.

Now, I feel like a little kid again, struggling with something as basic as keeping the bed dry.

***

The day of Daddy's wedding finally arrives.

We're all in hustle-bustle mode. Daddy's KLA 320 is washed and sparkling clean. He has arranged a driver for the car because Daddy's getting the VIP treatment today. He will be taken to Church in his friend's car.

The morning sun is barely up, and Daddy's already giving the new driver a crash course on the car. But oh boy, the driver is struggling to get things right.

You see, this Standard 10 car is like the odd one out in the car world. Its gear lever is like a metal giraffe neck sticking out from the engine. To hit reverse, you must give it a little lift first. It's like the car's got its secret handshake.

The driver says he's driven every other car except the Standard 10.

Meanwhile, we cousins have this inside joke that Daddy's car only listens to Daddy.

The clock is ticking. We have to reach the Church soon.

In the end, Daddy decides to take matters into his own hands. And he drives the car himself to the Church.

The wedding and reception are done, and now I have my new Mummy.

I realise she is a loving person with big expressive eyes and a caring attitude.

And just as I start feeling happy, I hear that Granny is leaving for Kottayam. She won't be staying with us anymore.

***

During the weekend, we get back from Kottayam after dropping Granny at her home. And the house feels different.

My new Mummy is a good person. So everything that my Mummy told me is coming true.

I look up at the wall, expecting to see Mummy's picture next to Daddy's, like always.

But the beautifully framed picture is gone.

That picture of Mummy was a regular source of consolation for me whenever I wanted to see her face.

I must ask Daddy and find out who has removed it.

Daddy returns from work in the evening. But for some reason, I can't get myself to ask him.

After dinner, when I lie down to sleep, I miss Granny's presence. I miss our prayer time stories. I miss the scent of oil on her body.

How I wish Granny hadn't gone away to Kottayam. I could have asked her about the missing photograph.

My heart feels heavy with so many questions. And I'm gradually realising that a lot more has changed than what I was told.

I lie with my eyes wide open, watching the fan swirl noisily above. And now I know what it feels like to be all on my own.

But I must not remain sad. Didn't Mummy tell me to be a brave and obedient boy?

After all, who needs a photograph when you have such vivid memories of the good times with Mummy?

And no one can take them away from me.

## Passage 27: Who Moved My Lunch Box?

New Place, New Friends, New Thrills

Daddy says he's planning to start a shop to sell lunch boxes. And I will be his biggest customer.

You see, my Daddy's got a heart of gold.

He doesn't punish me or give me a good whack like some dads do. Instead, he prefers to hit me with sarcasm when I lose yet another lunch box.

Nowadays, I'm in a hurry to get back home from school. I've made lots of friends in the neighbourhood.

And in the evenings, we transform a neglected patch of land next to an office building into a football battlefield.

So, when that final school bell rings, I'm on a mission to bolt out of there faster than P. K. Banerjee taking a penalty shot for the Indian football team.

But in my mad dash to pack up my books, I keep leaving my lunchbox behind. It's only when I get home and peek into the kitchen that it hits me like a football smashing on my face: "I forgot my lunch box… again."

Mummy likes to threaten me, warning me that I will have to go to school the next day without lunch. I can't argue, though, because it's my fault for being so forgetful.

And maybe also because I don't want to annoy her more than I already do.

She already finds many of the things I do irritating. I don't even know why. Even when I try not to make a fuss, she finds some reason to say I'm being careless or noisy or lazy.

The next morning, when I pack my school bag, I spend anxious moments. Will I get lunch today? A school bag without a lunchbox is so meaningless.

But just when I'm about to accept my fate as the poor, hungry boy without lunch, Mummy swoops in with a smile and hands me a new lunchbox.

It's way smaller than my usual jumbo stainless steel one, but hey, at least it's something, right?

Daddy keeps buying me more lunch boxes, but this time he's got me an aluminium one. The aluminium lunch box looks unpleasant when compared to the smart stainless steel ones.

And to make matters worse, he warns me that if I lose this one, I'll get an even smaller and shabbier replacement.

Some of my classmates bring aluminium lunch boxes, but they're all rectangular and perfect for sandwiches.

Me? I'm all about the big round stainless steel ones. I need lots of space for my rice and curry, after all.

Opening my lunchbox during lunchtime is always thrilling.

There's almost always a big, glorious piece of fried fish in there. That's why, when it's lunchtime, I don't want to chat with anyone or show off what's in my lunchbox. Sharing? Nah, not my style.

Whether I remember to bring back my lunchbox or not, when it's time to play, a kid needs to play.

So off I run to our playground.

I'm the goalie, the fearless protector of my stone goalposts.

We don't have fancy real goalposts, so our goalposts are made up of stones. And I dive from one stone to another like my hero, Goalie Thangaraj.

Daddy took me to a real football match once in Maharajas College Ground, and that's when I saw the legend himself, Goalie Thangaraj, in action. And I am sure that he can stop a bullet if it were kicked at him.

Today, it's an exciting game, and neither team has scored. Then, out of nowhere, the ball rockets towards me.

I make a Thangaraj-style leap and make a spectacular save.

My team and the boys watching the game go wild!

I toss the ball high and strike it with all my strength... just like Goalie Thangaraj. And the ball swishes through the air like magic.

Everyone's cheering, clapping, and then...**CRASH**!

A loud, sharp **BOOM**!

An office window explodes into tiny shiny pieces. The wooden frame bangs back against the wall like it saw a ghost.

After the glass bits finish their dance on the concrete, it's suddenly quieter than a library, except for the frightened Pomeranian pup next door.

My heart is doing a rhythmic pounding in my ears.

Everyone's frozen. Eyes wide.

And my eyes dart around, trying to avoid blame. What will happen now?

Then—**bam**!

Two angry men burst out of the office like action heroes in reverse. No slow-motion. Just fast-motion fury.

They yell like someone's stolen their lunch. And they grab our ball.

"Go away!" one of them yells.

And we do. Fast. Heads down, feet moving.

But inside, I'm quietly happy.

They didn't ask us to pay for the window. Thank goodness.

So here we are, with no more football and nothing interesting to do.

The next day, Mummy can't believe her eyes.

I'm sitting at home instead of running wild with my gang. Usually, she's all about convincing me to stay inside, but today she's like, "Why aren't you outside?"

I was expecting that. I don't know why Mummy has to ask so many questions like these.

Anyway, I explain about the office guys telling we should not play there anymore. I'm sure it's better not to talk about the broken window.

I being at home drives Mummy nuts because I usually bother her when she's tuned in to her fancy PHILIPS transistor radio with an antenna that looks like it's ready to launch into space. And she protects it like a dragon guarding a big treasure.

You've got to position it just right to catch the signals. Sometimes it gets all cranky, and Mummy has to give it a little tap.

So now, I'm the official tapper. But she thinks I'll break her precious radio.

But hey, a kid's got to have some fun, right?

Now, anyway, the rainy season is starting, and I'll have to spend my evenings at home.

I have now started taking an umbrella to school.

And Daddy says he is already planning to start an umbrella shop next to the lunch box shop.

Funny Daddy!

And if it's not the lunch box I forget, it's the bus money.

Sometimes, after a good game of volleyball or football, I reach into my pocket and find nothing.

The 10 paise I need for the bus ride home has vanished. Gone. Lost in the excitement or maybe in the grass somewhere near the goalpost.

But I know exactly what to do. I just walk over to Usha Bakery.

Uncle there never says no.

He just smiles and gives me a 10 paise coin, no questions asked. I always say I'll return it the next day.

Sometimes I do. Sometimes I don't.

But he never reminds me. He never even hints.

It's like he knows what it feels like to be a schoolboy with empty pockets and a long way to go.

Sometimes I think I've taken 10 paise from him more times than I can count.

But he still smiles. Always.

I don't think I'll ever forget that kind of kindness.

It's like getting your lunch box back when you thought it was gone forever. Some people forgive quietly. Some people understand things without needing to say them.

But not everyone does.

***

I once heard Mummy telling a guest that I still wet the bed. She laughed, like it was a joke.

She doesn't know I heard her. And she doesn't know that I never used to.

I feel very ashamed about it. And I keep thinking maybe she's telling other people too. The visitors who come and smile at me make me nervous.

These days, I don't drink much water in the evenings. Just in case.

But sometimes, even that doesn't help.

Sometimes I wake up scared. And sometimes, I don't wake up in time.

You see, some people forgive without a word. Some understand things without needing an explanation. But not everyone.

Especially the ones who already believe I'm not quick enough. That I forget too much. That something about me is just… not quite right.

That's why I sometimes close my eyes and try to imagine I'm back in the village.

Where the river calls my name.

Where fear arrives not as shame, but as a story Granny tells to get us home before dark.

A story that makes you want to run, not hide.

## PASSAGE 28: THE CROCODILE THAT NEVER LEFT

Where River Stories Come Alive

Granny never needed to raise her voice twice.

If we refused to climb out of the river even after the sun started to dip and the bats began their flying practice, she would simply step out onto the verandah, her hands on her hips, and say it.

Loud enough for the whole river to hear:

"You want the crocodile to come and take you?"

That was all it took.

We'd spring out of the water like soap slipping from a hand.

Because we all knew the story.

Granny would tell us about the Great Flood of '99.

No, not 1999. The Malayalam calendar '99, which came way before I was born.

The river had risen so high that everyone thought the world would end in water.

It rained for days. Grandfather was still alive then, and our ancestral home had turned into a rescue shelter.

People from the nearby lower-lying lands moved into our home, soaking wet and terrified. Granny cooked huge pots of kanji and curry to feed everyone, including children and the elderly. The house was packed, but no one went hungry.

When the rains didn't stop, Grandfather made a decision: everyone would move to the attic.

But the attic didn't hold up for long. The flood was too stubborn.

So he brought in two country boats, huge ones meant for carrying coconuts and husks to far-off markets — and tied them together, making a floating house.

They cooked, slept, and waited in those boats, bobbing on the water, watching their lives float by.

And when the flood finally left, it left behind a guest.

A crocodile.

It was first spotted by a bunch of children near the far end of the river—right where the current slows down and old banana stems like to get stuck.

It was big, brownish-grey, and always kept its mouth wide open like it was waiting for a dentist.

Granny said it just floated around, mouth agape, snapping shut when something unlucky flew in. Kids even tossed bits of leftover food from the banks just to see the snap!

Clap! went the jaws, faster than a schoolteacher's scale.

And it became an instant celebrity.

Until one day, it vanished.

No one knew where it went. But Granny never forgot. And neither did we.

So when she warned us, we listened. Because what if the crocodile had never really left?

And besides, everything gets scarier in the dark.

Even rivers.

***

Every Saturday before our river bath, Granny would line me and my cousin up for our oil massage.

She used thick, cold coconut oil for our bodies and a darker, warmer one—boiled with herbs—for our scalps. That oil had a peculiar smell, one that always made me think of her. Earthy. Sharp. Somehow caring.

She'd press it into our heads with her knuckles, mumbling things like, "Don't go catching cold," and "This will make your bones strong." We'd squirm and laugh, but we never complained. Because the bath that followed was worth every minute of it.

The river glimmered in the morning sun, and our bodies would slip into it slick with oil, slicing through the water like fish.

***

Across the river lies our family's coconut drying ground.

Hundreds of coconuts lay out under the sun, and our job is to guard them from greedy hens. Crows we could scare with black flags on bamboo poles. But hens? They don't care.

So we sit on a little outpost made of coconut stems and thatched leaves—a sort of treehouse without a tree.

Legs dangling, chewing bits of dried copra, we watch the hens like hawks.

That perch belongs to PappachanChettan, the man who seems to run everything around the property.

He isn't just any helper—he's part of the family in many ways. Granny always treats him with a kind of quiet respect, and he, in turn, does a hundred things without being asked.

In the afternoons, he climbs up to that perch, lies down with one arm flung over his face, and snores softly above the coconuts… like a watchman in paradise.

When it's lunchtime, he eats rice and curry like a king.

His plate is always a small mountain of rice with ladles of gravy on top, and during tapioca season, he mashes up the boiled kappa with a grin that says this is real food.

And we always know that whenever we arrive from Ernakulam, he'll be waiting near the edge of the backwaters—pole in hand, balancing on the big country boat.

From the last motorable point to our ancestral home is still a long ride through winding water.

But with PappachanChettan guiding the boat, it always feels like a smooth slide back into a world where time doesn't chase you.

***

Near the edge of the coconut land is a large fishpond with a Chinese net. But we aren't allowed to fish unless my uncle decides the fish have grown big enough. No catching the little ones.

Occasionally, Uncle arranges a few strong men to haul in big country boats for maintenance. They smell like fish oil and salt and wood—a mix that made our noses wrinkle.

We aren't allowed near those boats. Not because they're sacred. Just dangerous. The way they are propped up, they could fall and crush someone. But still, from a distance, they look like sleeping whales.

Sometimes we'd wander to the far end of the land, to where thin strips of coconut groves were lined with small side-streams.

These water channels made the land look like a green maze. Walking there was thrilling… but also a bit nerve-racking. The grass grew tall and thick, and you couldn't always see what was hiding in it. And everyone knew snakes liked places like that.

So my cousin, the brave one, always went first.

I followed only when he gave me the signal.

We made sure to tell Granny before going that far. Because if she called and we didn't answer, the whole house would panic.

From the perch near the coconut yard, though, we could hear her perfectly. She'd shout across the river, and we'd shout right back, like human megaphones.

***

Sometimes, the water in those side streams would be drained by groups of bare-chested men using bucket-like scoops made from coconut fronds. They'd swing big pails tied to ropes and transfer water back to the river.

And when the last of the water was gone, the fish show would begin.

Fish flapping and flipping, mud flying. Some fish kept trying to bury themselves into the wet earth. It was chaos.

That night, the whole village smelled like Granny's red fish curry.

She cooked it in a huge pot, the kind that could feed a festival. The trick was to boil the curry every day so it stayed good all week. And it tasted better each time.

Even our dogs joined the feast. They roamed free, tails wagging. The grumpy one kept in the cage barked anyway, just to be part of the action.

But before bedtime, when the smell of fish faded and the lanterns were lit, we'd go quiet.

And someone—either my cousin or me—would whisper:

"What if the crocodile comes tonight?"

Granny didn't even have to answer. Her silence said enough.

It never really left. Not in her stories. Not in our minds.

## PASSAGE 29: BEEP-BEEP, BEEP-BEEP, YAY!

Some day you can drive my car

"It's quite expensive," says Mummy.

"But it's worth the investment," Daddy says. "It gives much better mileage."

"I like it," I say. It's fantastic".

It all started when Daddy decided to sell his old Standard 10 car, KLA 320, and got a sleek Fiat 1100D with the number plate KLE 6433.

This new car is more spacious and way smarter than the Standard 10.

And the best part? It has the gear lever on the steering column! None of that awkward giraffe-neck gear-shifting nonsense!

KLA 320 was an ancient and sleepy car without a spirit or sense of adventure.

Only Daddy could drive it. It was like a one-driver-only car that would revolt if anyone other than Daddy tried driving it.

And by some miracle that no one has ever been able to explain, we used to travel back and forth between Kottayam and Ernakulam every week.

Must be Granny's prayers.

I am happy that we sold it. But a little worried that the new owner may bring it back to Daddy, complaining that nothing works well in the car.

I've never been interested in helping Daddy wash the KLA 320, but this new car is a thriller. I enjoy walking around and sitting inside the car whenever I can.

So I convince Daddy that I am the car-washing genius he never knew existed.

After some persuasion, he reluctantly hands me the sponges and soap.

One morning, as I finish scrubbing the car, I settle myself into the driver's seat.

And I do all my usual imaginary driving by turning the steering wheel and changing the gears. The gear shifts so perfectly and without the comedy of the gear of the Standard 10.

And then a spark hits me. Why not warm up the engine for Daddy?

Daddy can just drive away immediately if I have already done the engine warm-up for him. Genius, right?

I've noticed that Daddy always shifts the gear to neutral when he starts the engine. So I shift the gear to neutral and insert the key into the ignition.

I turn the key and press the accelerator a bit. Vroom! The engine roars to life.

Just then, Daddy rushes out with half his face foamy like a runaway snowman, razor in hand.

With determination in my eyes, I declare, "Daddy, see, I can do it! I'm ready to learn to drive!"

Daddy finally shuts his gaping mouth. And his bulging eyes return to their sockets.

"Not now. Not yet", he says. "You're only thirteen."

Why is Daddy such a spoilsport? I wonder.

Anyway, in a few days, I jet off for my Summer Holidays to Granny's place in Kottayam as usual.

I'll let Daddy clean his car for two months while I'm away.

***

This time, I spend more time with my elder cousins in their house. They have way more action going on.

Granny's not too happy about it. She thinks I'm still a small boy who needs constant supervision.

My daily routine now includes trips to Kottayam town with Sunnychayan in his fancy Fiat.

He gets his car outfitted with all the latest gadgets and accessories from Coimbatore.

He has a classy stereo with an aerial that does a dance and windows that move up and down at a button's touch.

The seats are plusher than a king's throne.

Sunnychayan looks so smart when he lights his cigarette from the cigarette lighter on the stylish dashboard, when it pops out with a burning glow.

Daddy's car is missing out on all this stylishness. I must let him know this.

***

When in town, I hang out at Sunnychayan's bakery.

Sunnychayan is always mingling with customers and friends. And he wants me to be at the cash counter.

It's so much fun to collect money from customers and give them the exact amount of change.

And when the urge strikes, I sneak into the back room, where the broken biscuit tins await. These have a special place in my heart, thanks to Sunnychayan and Rajuchayan, who used to bring them to my boarding school.

At noon, Sunnychayan gives me a handsome allowance for taking care of the cash counter.

With that money, I strut into the Rajadhani Hotel like a king in his palace. The steaming rice, drenched in seasoned buttermilk, accompanied by curries, makes your taste buds do a happy dance.

In the afternoons, my cousin Sajuchayan and I walk across to Babuchayan's shop, where he sells electrical fixtures.

We hound Manichettan, Babuchayan's driver, with questions about driving. He has some thrilling stories about his drives to Coimbatore in Babuchayan's jeep.

Finally, one bright evening, we charm Babuchayan into letting us drive his Ambassador in an empty field opposite his shop.

Everything about this car is like the Fiat, only bigger and with a gear that felt like it was always on vacation.

Our initial attempts resemble a comedy of jerks and sudden stops, making spectators flee to safety.

After we stumble through several such lessons, we're itching to hit the real road. But Babuchayan cautions us about the legal aspects.

That changes one day when Manichettan has to take Babuchayan to the Thiruvarppu Panchayat Office.

Babuchayan leaves us in the car as he goes inside.

Waiting in a parked car is such a waste of time. "Manichettan, can we at least reverse the car?" I plead.

With Babuchayan's reluctant approval, I engage the gear and backup like a pro. But then, attempting to shift into first gear, the car rolls back in reverse and hits the Panchayat building ramp.

Panic!

But Babuchayan stays cool.

He knows a guy at the Panchayat Office. A few words, and suddenly, it was like it never happened.

Lesson learned: Charm and connections can smooth over even government property mishaps. So I must practice being more charming with Daddy so that I can smooth over his reaction when he hears about this.

## Passage 30: First Day First Show

Two months is too less for summer holidays

Thursdays, oh, the glorious anticipation!

Why, you ask? Well, it's simple: the next day is Friday – the new movie release day.

You see, my cousin Sajuchayan and I belong to the First-Day First-Show Club.

Sajuchayan is my guide during every summer holiday in Kottayam since he's a year older than me and happens to live here.

Thankfully, our little town of Kottayam boasts not one, not two, but five theatres. Rajmahal, the classic one with no air conditioning, Anupama, the fancier one, and the triple treat – Anand, Asha, and Abhilash.

Often, it's so difficult to choose which movie deserves our "first show on the first day" treatment.

Of course, we must rely on the wisdom of the posters plastered all over town. And if we'd been lucky, we would have seen a trailer during a previous cinema interval.

***

Friday morning, we grab the newspaper and inspect the list of movies released in the theatres. We can't risk any last-minute surprises, you know.

So, after a delightful lunch at the Rajadhani Hotel, we dash to the cinema.

Running a famous bakery makes Sunnychayan well-known throughout the town. So the theatre managers are buddies with him.

That's why even if we're trying to grab tickets for a house-full show, it's easy. A phone call from Sunnychayan opens doors usually locked with "Sold Out" signs.

During the movie's interval, we wriggle our way through a sea of people, all scrambling to get their hands on refreshments and cigarettes like they've been stranded in a desert for days. But the trouble is worth it when we sip our chilled Fanta.

Finally, when the movie's credits roll and the lights come on, we rush back to provide Sunnychayan with a detailed review. But not before a quick Bombay Toast and Coffee from Best Bakers Restaurant, where our regular waiter, Mohammed, serves us in a jiffy with a broad smile.

Occasionally, we plan to sneakily catch more movies without telling Sunnychayan.

Of course, such missions are impossible at Rajmahal, where Manager Kuruvilla practically has a permanent residence in Sunnychayan's bakery. The man can't resist a daily chat with my cousin.

So, our plan usually involves watching the first couple of movies at Rajmahal and Anupama and playing it safe. Our secret missions occur at the three-in-one theatres – Anand, Asha, and Abhilash.

But no matter how careful we are, it's like Kottayam town has an invisible gossip network. Either Sunnychayan, Babuchayan, or Rajuchayan always gets to know.

Having three local businessmen as cousins has its disadvantages too.

You can run all you want in Kottayam, but you can never hide from your cousins.

***

On Sunday mornings, we're dragged to church by Granny.

"Are you coming to my place, dear?" she asks while exiting the Church.

"Not today, Valliammachi. I'll come after a couple of days". I like living with my Valliammachi. But I don't want to miss my daily trips to Kottayam town with my elder cousins.

***

You already know about my Aunty—the one with the three big sons who act like breakfast kings every morning, shouting for extra eggs and more sugar in their coffees.

She's the sweetest person on this planet.

She lost her hearing in both ears after delivering her fifth child. But that hasn't dulled her at all.

Her cooking is like magic.

Aunty feeds her husband (my Daddy's eldest brother), three sons, and two daughters like it's a feast every day.

And let's not forget the guests and relatives who drop by unannounced. She insists no one leaves without a full belly, and that includes the three household help she's got for taking care of the cows and the tilling and cultivation of the land attached to the house.

The joyful satisfaction radiating from her eyes when we enjoy her food is straight from her heart.

My Mummy used to say Aunty's spicy-red fish curry was the best in the world.

She relished every tiny bit, even the sun-dried Malabar tamarind and those wrinkly curry leaves in the dish.

So, when I sit down to have the fish curry, memories of my Mummy wash over me.

If Aunty catches me with damp eyes, I blame the chillies.

"The curry is spicy. But I love it, Aunty," I say, moving my lips clearly so she can see.

And when she catches it, her smile returns, like sunshine after rain.

I think I've become a real lip-reading expert now, just by talking with Aunty every day.

***

Evenings at home are a battle of willpower—and the meatsafe is the villain in plain sight.

It's this tall wooden cupboard with mesh on the doors, just enough to let the smell of cakes and biscuits escape and drive you crazy.

Aunty, clever as always, has each leg of the meatsafe standing in a little bowl of water—to stop ants from sneaking in. To me, it looks less like a cupboard and more like it's wading through four tiny puddles, while I stand there drooling at the goodies inside.

But often, Aunty slowly approaches me with a big steel plate brimming with seasonal fruits. Since it's summertime, it's a mango festival. She settles down beside me on the verandah with a smile. And slices the juicy fruit into perfect bites for me.

Aunty nibbles on the overripe, misshapen parts and whatever's left on the mango seed.

I want her to have some good pieces with me. But she insists with a glimmer in her eyes that the imperfect bits are her favourite.

While I enjoy the mango slices, she inquires about her three sons, Sunnychayan, Babuchayan, and Rajuchayan.

She's eager for updates, and I'm her trusted source.

She's anxious about her boys. Are they doing well in business or just blowing smoke rings with too many cigarettes? What do they eat? And who are their friends?

I've got the details, and Aunty, well, she's got my heart.

When she listens, her eyes sparkle with the interest and concern of a mother who struggles to know how her grown-up children are doing.

No one seems to spend enough time with her to communicate patiently. And I can sense the isolation she feels due to her deafness.

She reminds me of how caring my Mummy was. Always concerned. Always loving.

I'm going to miss all of this because Daddy is coming soon, since my summer holidays are coming to an end.

And then it's back to school in Ernakulam.

Why does time have to fly so fast in Kottayam?

## PASSAGE 31: HOW COOL WAS YOUR SUMMER?

Where fun ends, enthusiasm takes over

Man, it's like an oven in here!

But even in this scorching heat, hanging out at Sunnychayan's Borma is a blast.

The walls are as black as coal. Blame it on those ovens, the hidden superheroes that bake bread and turn the walls into a canvas of coal art.

I watch the workers spread blazing coconut shell coals inside the oven until it's hotter than a dragon's breath. And I can feel the sizzling heat on my skin.

The bread baked here is so fluffy and delicious that I can gobble a whole loaf in one go!

But hold on, Saturdays are the jackpot.

Master baker Sukumaran whips up a special dough for a special bread every Saturday. It's like the superhero of bread– longer, fancier, and with more dried fruits than a fruit salad at a fancy party.

Sunnychayan is like the guardian of this super bread and guards the exact number of these beauties.

But the master baker sets aside a wee bit of that special dough mix just for us to taste. And let me tell you, it's fabulous!

After my special bread party at the Borma, I walk across to the Bakery. And Sunnychayan says Daddy's in town.

Shucks! My two months of summer freedom are coming to an end.

***

Fast forward to closing time, we're rolling back to Thiruvarppu with K.J. Jesudas, the golden voice of Malayalam music, doing his best to sing our sorrows away on the stereo.

Usually, I'm the chatterbox. But today I'm stuck in "Farewell to Freedom" mode, dreading the return to Ernakulam.

We're almost home when Sunnychayan realises he's low on cigarettes. Normally, he'd grab some from the village shop, but this time, both my Uncles would be in the tea shop next to this shop. And that's a no-go zone.

This is where my Uncles have their bottles of toddy brought to them to their regular spot inside the tea shop, because they can conveniently enjoy their drink without having to visit the noisy toddy shop.

But we're on a cigarette mission here. So we park.

I take a deep breath and walk towards the tea shop. I flash Sekharanchettan, the tea shop owner, my best "I'm-an-innocent-teenager" smile. And casually ask if he's seen my Daddy passing by.

"Yes. Kunjachan (My Daddy) is inside with Kunjunju and Kuttappan (My Uncles)".

It's funny that every one of the older generations seems to be known only by their pet names in the village.

Daddy comes to me with a happy grin, smacking the drops of toddy from his lips.

While I casually chat with Daddy about our grand return plans, Sunnychayan sneaks off and gets the cigarettes from Sekharanchettan. Mission accomplished!

We share a laugh so loud it echoes across the river as we stroll home, crossing the creaky wooden bridge.

As we pass the toddy shop, it's like a full-blown concert – folks singing folk songs, banging on tables like there's no tomorrow, and keeping the good vibes rolling.

Just another evening in this village paradise. Lucky people!

***

The next day, Daddy and I say goodbye to everyone after the Sunday Church services.

Driving back to Ernakulam, I talk about the cool accessories that are missing in Daddy's car when compared to Sunnychayan's car.

Daddy doesn't seem interested. Too bad he can have only what originally came with the car.

***

This year, I get to upgrade from shorts to long trousers for school.

I get Navy Blue cloth for trousers and white cloth for shirts from the Bombay Dyeing showroom. And I trot over to my regular tailor, John Chettan, at Kombara Junction.

It's a disappointment that I can't wear bell-bottom trousers because PT Master would throw a fit. He once shouted at a boy for wearing flared pants, like it was some kind of crime.

Still, I do have one set.

Sunnychayan got me a white-and-green checked stretch-cloth from his friend Aliyar, who sells imported stuff. John Chettan stitched it into proper bell-bottoms… flares and all. And sometimes, when no one's looking, I try it on and imagine walking into a movie scene. Too flashy for school, of course. So it stays in my cupboard, waiting for its big day.

For now, I've got more serious business… like getting a new tiffin box and umbrella before school starts again.

***

I'm not thrilled any more about taking the Bus to school. A bicycle would be great, but getting a "yes" from Daddy feels like a journey to Mount Everest.

Still, I won't give up. Persistence is my middle name.

On the first day of School, everyone is in a new set of uniforms and happy to meet each other after two months of summer holidays.

The morning assembly starts with a prayer. And then our Principal, Mr. V.V. Achunny, goes on and on about his favourite word "Enthusiasm". If he had his way, he would start and end each sentence with the word "enthusiasm".

Initially, it took a while for everyone to understand when he said "ENDHOO…ZIAA…ZUM"

Principal Achunny finally runs out of steam, but just when we think we're in the clear, he drops the bombshell that our classmate PP George is going to perform a mono-act.

Now, PP has been performing his mono-acting everywhere, and Achunny, seeing PP's enthusiasm, gives him a license to "entertain" us.

But the backbenchers – me, Raghuram, and Feroz – have had enough of PP's one-man show. It's time for Operation Mono-Act Control, a top-secret plan destined for success.

We just have to execute it like super-spy commandos.

## Passage 32: Prankensteins Of The Back Bench

Frankly, it's just a prank

"Hey, can I get 25 paise?"

PP George is in a generous mood. And promptly hands over a coin to Raghuram.

PP's been on a roll lately, you see. He just got back from this mono-act competition, and man, you'd think he won an Oscar. He's been gabbing about how he should've won first prize instead of third.

Our gang of backbenchers is used to this routine whenever PP returns from a competition.

He goes on and on, bragging about the crowd that cheered for him, claiming he got more applause than the guy who nabbed first place.

We exchange glances, not sure whether to laugh or roll our eyes. We know better than to burst his bubble.

After what feels like an eternity of self-praise, PP moves on to his next audience, leaving us in peace.

All of us at the backbench are exhausted from PP's bragging.

Don't we deserve to have some fun? So, we put our genius minds together and hatch a plan.

We buy an inland letter from Kadavanthra Post Office with the 25 paise coin we took from PP.

We fill the letter with compliments and admiration. And sign it off as Sunila, a mysterious admirer. We also add a hint of romance just enough to tug at PP's heartstrings.

In the letter, Sunila raves about how PP deserved the first prize, practically declaring her undying love for his acting skills. She even suggests that if she were the judge, he'd be the undisputed winner.

When the letter arrives, PP's eyes light up like a Christmas tree. He parades Sunila's letter proudly in front of our teachers, especially Marar Madam, relishing the praise from this mysterious admirer. Things are getting out of control fast, and we can't keep up the act any longer. So we pull PP aside and spill the beans.

We watch PP's heart shatter into a thousand pieces when he eventually accepts the truth.

Fuelled by frustration, PP goes to Marar Madam and admits that it was all a prank.

She unleashes a torrent of words about the idiocy of our actions.

We stand there, heads hung low, faces drenched in regret.

But in the end, she forgives us. Phew!

***

Meanwhile, our ever-enthusiastic Principal Achunny is all about morning school assemblies. He's always inviting guests to motivate us into increased levels of "enthusiasm".

One day, it's a Malayalam film director and everyone's rapt with attention.

After the talk, Principal Achunny reveals the next agenda item: a mono-act by none other than PP. We groan in unison.

PP does his usual routine, and then, after the assembly, he starts tailing the Film Director like a detective on a mission.

When the director finally leaves, PP returns with the biggest grin, claiming he impressed the guest.

The very next day, Raghuram tricks PP into handing over another 25-paise coin.

And sure enough, a letter arrives a few days later.

Lo and behold, it's from the film director himself! He praises PP's talent and offers him a role in his next movie.

PP goes berserk, spreading the news like wildfire.

We keep our mouths shut, thinking they'll eventually figure out it's another prank.

But there's no way they can trace it back to us. We've written it in different handwriting and sprinkled some fancy English words to sound professional.

But PP drops a bombshell on us: PT Master's about to report the letter to the Principal, and he'll announce the good news in tomorrow's assembly.

Uh-oh. Panic mode gets activated.

We corner PP and confess that this letter was another prank.

He doesn't believe us because he's already started visualising himself as a superstar actor.

So we quickly recite the exact contents and finally convince him it's our handiwork.

I take responsibility for this since I wrote the letter, although with some help from Peter George, our vocabulary wizard. Just that Peter had no clue that the big words he had supplied would make their way into a prank letter.

We pay the price for our mischief, standing outside for hours and getting a lecture about the legalities of impersonation.

Thankfully, PP vouches for us, saying it was just a prank and that he has no complaints against his friends.

But PT Master pulls me aside and reminds me about my dad's friendship with him from college days and how my Mummy would be disappointed if she were alive.

From the burning earnestness in his eyes, I know he means every word he's saying.

I dare not meet his sharp gaze. And I don't want to reveal my defencelessness by shedding tears.

He goes on lecturing. But my ears are deafened by the voices in my head echoing the stinging words he said earlier.

He may be right. But I hate him for making me look irresponsible and reckless in front of the whole school.

Not on my life must I allow the students passing by to see my eyes drenched in tears.

I have worked hard to bury memories of my Mummy deep within me, and I must not let them resurface as tears in front of anyone.

After PT Master scolds me to his heart's content, I inch towards the classroom, burdened with guilt and shame. And I feel like a total loser.

All the backbenchers stare anxiously at my face as I enter the classroom. Their eyes follow me closely while I silently slump into my seat with the weight of bitter resentment.

Just then, PP declares in his dramatic flair that he'll never lend us a 25-paise coin again. And we all burst into laughter.

Yeah, we'll have to endure more of his mono-acts.

Blame it on "ENDHOO...ZIAA...ZUM"

## PASSAGE 33: SCHOOL OF HARD KNOCKS

As strong as Hercules

Hey, you won't believe it! I finally got myself a bicycle.

But hold onto your handlebars, because this isn't some shiny, out-of-the-box ride.

Nope, I had to rummage through Daddy's shop and pick one from a bunch of dusty, old bikes in the corner.

See, I had my eyes on this ultra-cool BSA bike at the Broadway Cycle Shop.

But I had to hit the brakes on the drooling over that gleaming cycle when life decided to surprise me with a Hercules instead.

This Hercules bike is like the big, friendly giant of bicycles, not as sleek as the BSA. But I'm starting to like its sturdiness.

Because now I can rule the streets, one bumpy road at a time!

As I cruise towards school, I spot Rao Sir pedalling away on his bicycle.

I can zip past him in the blink of an eye, but there's a tiny problem. I've committed the ultimate crime of not doing my homework.

So, I'd better slow down and enjoy the show as he wobbles from side to side, stretching like a rubber band as he tries to reach the pedals.

A tricycle would be ideal for him. Now, this is what I call the daily morning entertainment!

Homework is so boring, and I'm not wasting my time on it.

Fast forward to Sanskrit class, and Ramakrishnan Sir begins chanting mystical Sanskrit incantations —long strings of ancient words that swirl through the air like invisible smoke.

He stands tall at the front of the class, like a wise sage from an old temple calendar. His lean frame is always draped in a neatly pressed shirt; it looks like even the fabric respects him.

His black-rimmed glasses sit calmly on his nose, giving him the permanent look of someone who's just read something very serious.

He's quite pleasant most of the time. Smiles politely. Doesn't yell. It's just that his subject feels less like a language and more like a secret code.

And all I can barely decipher is that Sanskrit is essentially Hindi with a couple of dots placed mysteriously to the right of a vowel.

Ramakrishnan Sir usually aims all his attention at the front-row geniuses. We backbenchers are left in peace, free to doodle heroic stick figures or dream of lunch.

Until today.

"Mohan!" he says.

Who dares disrupt my doodling in peace?

Oops! It's Ramakrishnan Sir.

He is now staring straight at me. He wants to inspect my homework.

I stand up, give my famous "I'm-sorry-please-don't-kill-me" head rub with my right hand and mumble, "I forgot, Sir…"

Some kids giggle. I see the front-row boys exchange smirks. But I try to look innocent, like a poor victim of sudden memory loss.

He lets the class savour the moment and quips, "Don't go '*porogoat*' (Malayalam for backwards), come '*mumboat*' (Malayalam for forward)."

The class erupts. Even I can't help smiling. I've officially made an ass of myself, but in style.

He pats me gently on the shoulder and says, "Next time, take your homework seriously."

And just like that, I escape.

Phew! That was too easy.

Next up—the dreaded Mathematics class.

Enter Rao Sir.

The moment he steps in, the whole room tightens. Laughter dies, spines straighten, and even the ceiling fan seems to slow down in fear.

Rao Sir is short, round like a tea kettle, with a massive paunch that arrives a full second before the rest of him.

His shirt buttons look like they're holding on for dear life.

His eyes? Always red. Not sleepy red, angry red.

He walks in like a man who's deeply disappointed by everything around him... including the very air we breathe.

His mouth is a permanent frown, and he looks ready to explode at the tiniest mistake.

And when he does explode, his weapon of choice is the whiteboard duster. Not the soft kind. The heavy, wooden one that feels like it was made during British rule.

We, the backbenchers, huddle in silence. Praying for invisibility. Hoping the gods of math will spare us today.

No such luck.

Rao Sir's eagle-red eyes scan the class, and then lock on to me.

"Homework!" he barks.

I slowly rise, trying not to tremble too obviously.

I summon all my courage, scratch the back of my head, and deliver my signature line:

"I forgot, Sir."

There's a small ripple of giggles from the class. But even they know—this is not going to end well.

He grabs my head while lifting his other hand as if to slap me. And with a mocking glare, he banishes me to the hallway.

"Bring a letter from your father, or stand outside forever", he yells.

***

Daddy, after a brief lecture, scribbles me a letter.

The next day, I stand proudly outside Rao Sir's class, clutching the letter.

As he walks in, I tell him I have brought the letter. But he shuffles past, completely ignoring me.

The minutes move on, and the class is due to end very soon. Still, he doesn't acknowledge my existence.

And I can't take the humiliation anymore.

I rip the letter into a million pieces and watch them flutter and twirl down to the ground floor where the School Bus is parked.

Ah, that felt good!

In a few minutes, the bell rings, and Rao Sir walks out. And he wants to see the letter.

Now, how am I supposed to hand over the letter when it's scattered all over the School Bus Shed?

His bloodshot eyes pierce my gaze.

"Sir, the letter flew down with the wind", I say, showing him how the wind had come and grabbed the letter away while I watched helplessly.

"Go get it", he snaps while lifting his hands as if to slap me.

So I spend a few minutes downstairs, pretending to search for the elusive letter.

The next day, I wait for Rao Sir outside his class, ready to deliver the bad news.

Rao Sir doesn't say a word at first. He just stares at me with those red, permanently furious eyes.

Then, with the speed of a reflex, his thick fingers grab hold of my head like he's opening a stubborn jam jar.

**THUD. THUD. THUD.**

The whiteboard duster meets my skull... wooden edge first.

I see stars.

Like, actual blinking stars.

One for each knock.

Maybe even a few planets.

That, my dear friends, is the only math I've learned in Rao Sir's class — counting planets while getting whacked.

In all this time, I haven't ever received physical punishment at home.

Especially my dear Mummy had a way of managing me without having to inflict physical punishment.

Yet, Rao Sir is surely making up for it.

But you see, I am strong and sturdy enough to handle the bumps like my trusted Hercules.

## PASSAGE 34: BURIED IN A HEAP OF COCONUTS

The drive to drive

I must say, Daddy is one lucky fellow.

Who else can score a daily, cost-free car wash that rivals a sparkling diamond, thanks to a highly motivated young chap like me?

The enthusiasm in my morning cleaning routine knows no limits, even when the car's already spotless.

Our car practically beams with happiness after my meticulous washing and thorough interior cleaning ritual. It's like a spa day for automobiles.

After all the buffing and scrubbing, I make sure everything under the bonnet is purring like a contented kitten. I've even got reverse parking down to an art form, much to Daddy's raised eyebrow of approval.

Of course, no one's spilt the beans to him about that one time I reversed Babuchayan's car into the Panchayat office wall. Fortunately, my cousins are keeping their lips sealed.

To be fair, it wasn't entirely my fault. It was a pretty steep slope, you see.

I decide that my car-caring skills have earned me the privilege of a spin on the Fiat during school holidays.

My favourite destination? The Tata Oil Mills compound.

It's just a short distance away, and that's where my buddy T. Sunil resides.

When I pull up and shout "Suniilll!", it's like a neighbourhood alarm clock, and everyone knows the daredevil has arrived.

Sunil's sisters giggle, and Sunil pretends to be embarrassed, but hey, I'm on a mission.

I rev the engine, flash a hero's grin, and park slightly crooked but with full confidence.

I may not be old enough to drive legally.

But by God, I drive dramatically.

As much as I've improved my driving skills, Daddy refuses to let me take the wheel on our weekly Kottayam trips. I've got four more years to wait for that driver's license.

The Fiat has now become our family's trusted travel companion, and we have smoother and puncture-free journeys to Kottayam.

Mummy's not a fan of Kottayam's wooden bridges, especially in the rainy season, so she usually stays home.

Lately, cousin Daiechayan's been living with us in Ernakulam, hoping to learn the ropes from Daddy for his business venture.

Our Kottayam trips now comprise Daddy, Daiechayan, and me.

Daiechayan insists on the front seat, which suits me fine since Daddy's playing it safe in the rain. I get to enjoy the lush roadside views better from the back.

When it's time to head back to Ernakulam, PappachanChettan's a pro at loading the Fiat's trunk with rice sacks, coconuts, and bushels of bananas and plantains, all cultivated on our family land.

Seeing these goods loaded takes me back to the days when we had the Standard 10 and changing punctured tyres was a family affair. I would help pull out a coconut at a time to help Daddy access the spare tyre.

Thankfully, the Fiat spared us such troubles.

We're driving back to Ernakulam in light drizzle, cruising steadily since we know this road so well. And we're just about to hit Vaikom town.

Rainwater-filled ditches line the road, and the rain has painted the lush vegetation in breathtaking shades of green.

People may grumble about the weather, but nature's loving it.

We're cruising along in the Fiat, tyres slicing through puddles, when suddenly, out of nowhere, a boy on a bicycle appears, wobbling straight into our path.

Daddy's reflexes kick in, narrowly averting a collision.

But the Fiat starts to skid.

Daddy battles to regain control, gears shifting, and the steering feeling useless.

The brakes are jammed. And we're skidding into oncoming traffic. And panic sets in.

Daddy leans into the horn — BEEEEEP! BEEEEEEP! — as if sheer volume might scare the truck away.

Screeching tires, honking horns, pounding hearts, and that terrifying sense of helpless chaos.

In an instant, the truck is getting bigger. And bigger.

And then — **BOOOOM**!

The world spins.

We slam into the front of the lorry and bounce right back into a waterlogged ditch, the Fiat landing with a splash.

For a few seconds, there's silence.

Then Daddy and Daiechayan turn around in slow motion.

Where am I?

All they see is a mountain of coconuts.

The partition between the trunk and the back seat has crumbled. And I'm buried in a heap of coconuts.

A few sturdy-looking men wade in and heave the car out of the ditch.

And we finally crawl out, dazed but alive. Our poor Fiat's front end looks like it lost a boxing match.

Relief washes over us as we read the name in bold letters on the lorry – Vellapally Brothers.

They are construction contractors, and Daddy knows them well.

Luckily, the lorry sustained only minor damage.

Turns out, it was built like a tank, and probably laughed at our poor little Fiat for even trying.

Yes, Daddy is one lucky fellow.

## PASSAGE 35: EATING LIKE A GIANT

Ace the race with grace

Games and sports, oh man, they're like a rollercoaster of fun that leaves your stomach growling for more.

You see, at home, it's all about hearty meals.

Mummy whips up huge portions of everything. And she insists on announcing to the whole world that I'm the insatiable eating machine.

To be honest, I can gobble down a massive bowl of rice that could easily feed a small army, but who's counting, right?

She's thinking I'm downing all that grub just for the fun of it.

No, sir! I need that fuel to power my daily bike races to school, to keep my trumpet sessions with the school band blowing strong, and to stay revved up for the wild world of sports and games I dive into.

Now, let's fast forward to the most exciting time of the year – the week leading up to the sports day.

We're out there, giving our all in every event under the sun, perfecting our long jumps like an art form.

But then, Anil Shivram shows up, like the ultimate wildcard, saying he wants to join in.

We exchange these knowing looks, thinking this guy's lung capacity is as good as a deflated balloon.

After all, this is the guy who taught us how to handle a cigarette – while five of us are casually puffing away at one shared cigarette, he inhales a whole cigarette like he's been training for it like a seasoned pro.

So here we are, preparing for a good laugh as Anil attempts a long jump.

He rolls up his trousers like he's about to wade through a puddle, and then, he defies gravity itself.

He leaps farther than any of us in the long jump, masters the high jump, and pole vaults over those bars like he's got some supernatural charm going on.

We're left scratching our heads, wondering if there's some smoky secret behind his awe-inspiring athleticism. It's like he's exhaling victory in perfectly round smoke rings.

Ah, how could I forget? This is the same Anil who cycles with me from school to Little Shenoy's theatre like the wind. Just to catch a matinee show.

Since attending the first class in the noon session is essential for getting attendance for the full day, we have to beat the clock to make it in time for the movie.

So, we're like secret agents, sneaking out through the side door, pedalling through the streets like rockets on fire, and securing those precious movie tickets like they're gold medals from the cycling Olympics.

So there's no way we'll ever miss a good Hollywood movie that hits town.

But hold on. It's time for the 10,000-meter cycle race. And for us, it's a walk in the park.

My trusty old Hercules may look like it's been around since the dinosaurs, but believe me, it's been pampered like royalty. Greased and tuned to perfection, and a set of fresh tires – we're ready to roll.

As the race unfolds, only a select few can keep up with our lightning pace.

I'm zooming through the bumps and troughs of the track and take the lead. I'm on my way to getting that first prize two years in a row.

But just then, for a split second, I glance back. And I spot my buddy PP right behind me.

The teachers are yelling, urging us to finish. But I do the unthinkable.

In a moment of friendship, I reach out a hand to PP. And together, we conquer the finish line.

It's like we just scored an Olympic double gold for friendship and sportsmanship.

***

Now, safety is the name of the game. Ever since that infamous javelin incident a couple of years back, when Nahas's javelin took a wild turn and punctured Kannan's thigh, we've learned our lesson.

It was like a scene from a suspense thriller, and it took the bravery of our teachers to rescue Kannan and get him to the hospital on the school bus.

Luckily, he made it out alive, even though he returned with a bit of swagger in his walk.

So, now, events like javelin, discus, and hammer throw come with a level of scrutiny that even Sherlock Holmes would appreciate.

No one wants another javelin incident on their hands. It's all fun and games until someone gets speared, right?

I'm famished as hell after all this excitement. And tonight again, Mummy is going to have to watch me polish off an entire bowl of rice all by myself.

I need to refuel for tomorrow, you see.

Right before the sports day prize distribution, we have to form a human pyramid. The strong and heavy guys form the base of this acrobatic tower, and we have to support multiple tiers of smaller boys on top of us.

We can't let them down. They trust that they're standing on the shoulders of giants, after all.

And for this, I must continue eating like a giant.

The Mummy in my life today—the one who came after—makes sure the meals are served on time, the house runs on routine, and life moves forward in order. Her care is steady, dutiful, and kind.

Yet, even as she places my plate before me, my heart still wanders… searching.

Searching for the Mummy I lost when I was ten.

The one who could make me feel safe with just a glance. The one whose love spoke in silence, through every small gesture—the warm meal waiting, the gentle touch on my head, the firm voice when I needed discipline.

She didn't laugh often, but her presence was unshakable. A smile was never far, and neither was her strength. She called me her "eating machine," and every extra spoonful she coaxed into me felt like her secret way of saying, you are loved.

Two women. Both called Mummy.

One who stepped in when life demanded it.

And one who never truly stepped out of my heart.

And so, in every bowl I finish, in every challenge I take on, in every moment I find myself strong—I know she is still here. Not gone. Not forgotten.

Just carried within me. Always.

MOHAN MATHEW CHACKO

**About this Epilogue:**

*A reflection from many years later—on the silence I chose, the love I buried, and the blessing I hope my daughter never overlooks.*

## EPILOGUE:

When Maria turned eleven, a hidden fear lifted. I had long carried the dread that she might lose her mother at the same age I lost mine.

The thought haunted me—not for myself, but for her. Because no father, no matter how devoted, can fill that void.

I kept this fear buried, but here it is now, written at last. If these words move even one reader to hold a mother closer, they've done their work.

When my mother left me, I was ten. And almost instinctively, I pushed her memory away. I hated the reminders, the sadness, the tears. I thought strength meant forgetting. So I forced myself not to remember.

But years later, the fragments returned—shards of love I could no longer deny. The physical cord was cut, but the emotional one never was.

I see now how much I lost, how much I miss her. Yet remembering no longer wounds—it steadies me.

So I write—for Maria, for my nieces and nephews, and for anyone who still has a mother. When you have it, you see the flaws. When it's gone, you see the treasure.

That truth is enough. And at last, I am at peace with it.

*If you're wondering how I remember so much, the truth is, sometimes life gently reminds me.*

## The Teacher, the Tea, and the Timeless Connection

A chance meeting that reminded me how memories find us, even when we aren't looking.

I wasn't trying to take a walk down memory lane that day.

I was simply trying to escape the boredom of a shop counter.

It was the 1980s. I had just joined my father's business—sanitary ware, plumbing materials, and tiles. His plan: learn the ropes, hold the fort, run the show.

My plan: anything but that.

That's how my Yamaha RD 350 became more than just a bike. It became my freedom pass. I convinced myself—and my father—that vendor registrations across Kerala were essential to our expansion. Armed with business cards, some youthful confidence, and an ever-ready pitch, I set off in search of potential clients.

One such day led me to the office of a tea plantation company. Grand gates, quiet prestige, and just enough mystery to keep my 22-year-old energy humming. I strode in, rehearsed smile in place. The receptionist barely looked up.

"We're not adding new vendors," she said flatly.

I stayed polite. A few minutes of persistence later, she said, "You'll have to meet the Company Secretary. If he agrees, it can be done."

At the time, I didn't know what a Company Secretary did. In my head, it sounded like someone with a notepad and a lot of free time.

I was wrong.

His office was all polished wood and quiet authority. The air smelled of tea and deliberation. I entered, pitched our product range, and spoke about quality and pricing. He listened carefully. Then looked at my card.

After a pause, he asked, "Where are you from?"

"Kochi," I said, casually.

"And your mother?"

That caught me off guard. "She was a teacher. She passed away when I was ten."

He sat back and smiled gently. "Did she teach in Calcutta?"

"Yes," I said, my curiosity rising.

"I knew it," he said, leaning forward. "She taught me in school. She was my favourite teacher."

The room changed in an instant.

What followed was not a business meeting, but a long, heartfelt conversation. He spoke of my mother the way old students speak of someone who shaped their world. With warmth. With laughter. With reverence.

"She wasn't just a teacher," he said. "She mothered us, encouraged us, made us feel seen. We never forgot her."

Then, with a smile: "And I remember your father too—waiting outside church, trying to win her over."

We both laughed. It was the kind of detail no son expects to hear during a business call.

He called for tea. And as we sipped, something quiet stirred inside me.

It had been so many years since she passed. But in that office, for those few minutes, it felt like she had returned.

When he said he'd approve our vendor registration, he added, "But you should know—it's not your pitch that got you this. It's her. She earned this for you, long ago."

As I rode home, the wind felt different. Softer. Like it was carrying her voice.

That day reminded me of something I've never forgotten since:

The world is small. But memory is even smaller.

It waits quietly, tucked into the people we meet, the things we don't expect, and the kindness we once received without realising its full weight.

Our loved ones may be gone. But they leave echoes—in the minds of strangers, in classrooms long dismantled, in tea shared decades later.

And if we're lucky, sometimes those echoes find their way back to us—when we least expect it, but perhaps when we need it most.

## FINAL NOTE: ONE LAST SLAP

A moment of discipline, a lifetime of love, and a farewell too soon.

I've lived a long life—stumbled through mistakes, taken wrong turns, ignored wisdom when I shouldn't have. And yet, if you ask me what I truly long for, it's not another chance to rewrite those mistakes.

It's something simpler.

Something impossible.

One last slap from my mother.

It must have been around 1965 or 1966. I was six years old—an obedient child, a rule-follower, someone who understood that 'no' meant 'no.' Mummy's word was law. No tantrums. No pleading. No negotiations. Life was simple. Life was safe.

Until the day I decided it wouldn't be.

Mummy was in the bathroom, the sound of the shower steady and rhythmic. And I, for reasons now lost to time, decided to test the one boundary I had always respected.

Maybe I wanted a toy. Maybe I just wanted her attention. Or maybe, for once, I wanted to see what would happen if I pushed back.

So I banged on the door.

Once. Twice. Over and over.

My little fists rattling the latch. My voice rising over the sound of the water.

She told me to stop. I didn't.

She warned me—firm and steady. I ignored her.

And then...

The latch gave way.

The door swung open, and I stumbled forward... skidding across the wet bathroom floor.

For a brief moment, I saw her... startled, caught off guard, her expression a mix of shock and concern I'd never seen before.

And then, before I could catch my breath...

A slap.

Sharp. Quick. Final.

Not out of anger. Not out of cruelty. But out of sheer instinct. A mother's instinct to protect, to correct, to teach.

I stood there, soaked and stunned. My six-year-old heart couldn't fully grasp it, but I knew... I had crossed a line.

I never got another slap from her.

Because four years later, she was gone.

Cancer came like a thief in the night... ruthless and unyielding.

But she fought it the way she fought everything… with quiet strength, unwavering resolve, and dignity that never broke. Even in pain, she didn't let me see her crumble.

And when the end came, I could almost hear her voice in my heart.

"You control your life, but don't forget your destiny."

"It's time to say goodbye. I know it will make you cry."

"You make your destiny. I know you'll find the way."

Outside, the sun was bright. It didn't seem fair. The world kept moving, unchanged, unaware of what it had lost.

But she was right. Life went on.

I walked my path. I stumbled. I failed. I grew.

And through all these years, I have felt the absence of that firm hand—that silent guardian who once corrected me when I needed it most.

I have deserved many slaps in life—for arrogance, for missteps, for forgetting who I was. But I never got another.

And now, after all these years, I find myself wishing for one last slap.

Not as punishment.

But as proof. Proof that she's still here.

Still watching. Still keeping me in line from somewhere I cannot see.

And who knows... When we meet again, I might just start an argument—just to see if she obliges.

Some instincts, after all, never fade.

## AUTHOR'S NOTE

When I began writing this memoir, I wasn't thinking about books at all.

I was thinking about memory—what lingers, what slips away, and how those fragments shape the person you become.

*You Told Me to Be Brave* is not a straight line. It's made of snapshots—of a boy growing up too soon, of a childhood stitched together with loss, awkwardness, small triumphs, and lessons learned the hard way.

Writing these pages was my way of honouring the emotions that refused to fade, even after all these years. At its heart, this book is not about perfect recollections. It is about what it means to keep going when the one person who made the world feel safe is no longer there.

Now, as a father, a husband, and still that boy who misses his mother, I offer these stories not as answers, but as a mirror—for anyone who has stumbled, carried too much, or searched for pieces of themselves in memory.

If these pages stirred something in you, I hope you'll share it. Not just this book—but your own stories, your own memories, your missing pieces.

Because in the end, stories—especially the quiet, personal ones—are how we keep those we love alive.

MOHAN MATHEW CHACKO

## Q&A WITH THE AUTHOR

**Q**: Why write this memoir now?

**A**: Because the story was waiting. Sitting quietly, nudging me to remember, reflect, and share. And maybe, just maybe, someone else would find a piece of themselves in it.

**Q**: There's humour woven throughout—was that intentional?

**A**: Absolutely. Life is messy. Even grief has absurd, ridiculous, and funny moments. Leaving them out would have been dishonest.

**Q:** The boy in the story has naïve, clumsy moments. Were those yours too?

**A**: Guilty! I stumbled, misjudged, and acted ridiculously at times. I wanted the memoir to feel real, not polished—a boy learning to navigate a world he didn't fully understand.

**Q**: What do you hope readers take away?

**A**: That resilience doesn't always roar. It whispers. It hides in laughter. It grows in quiet moments. Sometimes, it shows up in ways you never expect.

**Q**: If your mother could read this book, what would you want her to know?

**A**: That her words stayed with me. And that this is my way of keeping her alive in stories, not silence.

MOHAN MATHEW CHACKO

## A LITTLE NOTE BEFORE WE PART

Hey, it's me again.

You've just walked with me through some pages that mean the world to me.

I hope, somewhere along the way, you smiled, maybe sighed, maybe even remembered your own version of a "child who stumbled and grew."

I didn't write this book to be perfect. I wrote it to be human. To show that behind resilience were also naïve, clumsy, sometimes downright silly moments. Because that's what makes us real, isn't it?

If there's one thing I'd love for you to carry away, it's this: life shapes us in unexpected ways—and sometimes, the messiest chapters become the most meaningful.

**And one small favour?** If this story touched you at all, could you leave a rating and a short review?

Just a few honest lines. It's the single best hug you could give this little book before letting go.

Thank you, truly, for walking beside me. —Mohan

## About the Author

Mohan Mathew Chacko writes with the quiet clarity of someone who lived the story long before he found the words for it.

For years, he carried his memories silently—like unfinished sentences—while building a career in logistics and concept selling. But the urge to write never left.

It grew into a need: to give shape to the fragments, to honour what was lost, and to preserve what love had left behind.

You Told Me to Be Brave is his first memoir—a tribute to his mother and the echoes of her love that continue to guide him.

He lives in Kochi, India, with his wife Polly, and shares more stories and personal essays at his storytelling blog, WORDSOUPS, where memories, experiences, and creative thoughts find a home.

www.wordsoups.com

www.wordsoups.com.